HOW I PRAY

EDITED BY JIM CASTELLI

BALLANTINE BOOKS • NEW YORK

Library of Congress Catalog Card Number: 94-94359

ISBN: 0-345-38331-1

Cover design by Kristine Mills
Cover photo copyright © Dennis Hallinan/FPG International
Text designed by Debbie Glasserman

Manufactured in the United States of America
First Edition: October 1994
10 9 8 7 6 5 4 3 2 1

Praise for *How I Pray*

"Jim Castelli reminds us all that we are more alike than different when we pray. The shades of spirituality revealed here show how strikingly the same are our deepest human hungers. ... The insights found in *How I Pray* will contribute to religious cooperation and reconciliation."

> —James M. Dunn
> Executive Director
> Baptist Joint Committee

"A precious book ... A moving volume ... This lovely series of essays will give you new adventures, wonderful pilgrimages, and endless challenges. It might even bring you peace and tranquility you have never previously experienced."

> —Robert F. Drinan, S.J.
> Professor
> Georgetown University Law Center

"It was a delight and an inspiration to read the disarmingly honest and intimate thoughts of so many people on a subject that is often so difficult to talk about! A truly interfaith book, *How I Pray* encourages me to think that a world in which we respect one another as children of the same loving God is a real possibility."

> —The Rev. Barbara C. Crafton
> Author of *Finding Time For Serenity*

CONTENTS

ACKNOWLEDGMENTS

I want to thank the twenty-six people who told me how they pray. It's obvious that I couldn't have done this book without them, but they were real collaborators. Many took time out of their busy lives to talk to a stranger about very personal things, and I thank them for doing that. I also thank those people whom I already knew; they, too, spoke candidly about very private matters.

One of the things that made this project rewarding was that many of the people I interviewed were curious about how other people prayed. Now they can find out.

I spent a great deal of time asking people I respected—particularly journalists and religious leaders—to recommend people for me to interview. I could just as easily have written a book by interviewing the people I came to think of as my scouts: Art Winter, Dave Anderson, Bill Bole, Al Menendez, Kate DeSmet, Joan Connell, Clark Lobenstine, Robinna Winbush, Carol Fouke, Ken Briggs, Nick Van Dyke, Father Bud Kaiser, David Schaal, Frank Butler, Kim Lawton, David Neff, Tim Jones, Chuck Bergstrom, Jim Besser, Jim Rudin, David Saperstein, Jeff Hadden, Myrna Wahlquist, Jim Lewis, Ron Cruz, Dick Ostling, and John Borelli.

I'd also like to thank my wife, Jayne, for her advice and for her help in editing several of the transcripts.

PRAYING AND PRAY-ERS

Everyone prays. For some people prayer requires several hours a day and involves intricate rituals. For others prayer takes the shape of an occasional "Oh, no!" at bad news and "Thank God!" at good news.

Yet whatever the length, language, complexity, or faith of our prayers, they all ultimately have the same purpose: to reach outside of ourselves and touch, perhaps to move, a power greater than ourselves. We pray for mercy, for guidance, for forgiveness, for peace—both global and internal. Every time we pray, we acknowledge that there are things in this life that are outside of our control. Often we pray to bring about change in ourselves as well. Every time we pray, we try to become something more than we are.

Just as we strive for "excellence" in our professional lives, we strive for excellence, for improvement, for a way to come closer to that power or spirit in our prayer lives. But prayer is intensely personal and so we don't learn about prayer from dry treatises or lectures; we learn about it best from our own experience of it and from the stories of other people whose prayer is rooted in their own unique lives.

The purpose of this book is quite simple. I wanted to talk to a number of Americans from a wide variety of religious and professional backgrounds about their prayer lives—to ask them to fill in the blanks about "How I Pray." At one level their stories are fascinating in themselves, presenting a broad, multicultural portrait of American religion. Each story is an end in itself, telling us something about the role that prayer plays in people's lives, and how unique that role is in every instance. But these stories also provide an opportunity to discover themes and patterns in the way people actually pray, a chance to learn something about the generic nature of prayer.

The hard part was choosing the people to interview. I wanted not only a certain number of people who would be household names but also a good number of "real people," who were not necessarily big names outside their own households but who cared deeply about prayer. I wanted as broad a representation of religious groups as possible. I wanted, as much as possible, to interview people who were at least somewhat comfortable talking about their spiritual lives. I wanted religious leaders and laypeople. I wanted a group of people that reflected demographic diversity—by gender, age, race, ethnicity, region. At times I felt like Bill Clinton trying to assemble an administration that "looks like America"—only he had three thousand political appointees to work with while I had to pick fewer than thirty people to keep this book's size manageable.

My choices eventually reflected a combination of detailed planning and occasional whimsy. I picked some people because I knew pretty much what they would say, and I chose others because I had no idea what they would say.

After I conducted each interview, I transcribed it and edited it into a narrative so that each person would speak directly to the reader; I tried to keep these narratives as conversational as possible. That wasn't easy, particularly with the academics. But I thought it was important to make these stories as personal as possible, and our conversation is often much more personal than our writing.

The responsibility for the final interview choices is mine, and here's how I made them:

Phil Bom teaches at Pat Robertson's Regent University. I met Phil, a Presbyterian and an Evangelical, at a conference on religion and politics about two weeks before the 1992 election. I was struck by the fact that when Phil asked those present to pray for the presidential candidates, he did so in such a way that I couldn't tell whom he would vote for. That was refreshing, as was his visible enthusiasm about prayer.

Sidney Callahan is a popular and prolific Catholic writer who frequently writes about issues involving family and values. I was glad to interview her as I've enjoyed her writings for more than twenty years.

Joan Campbell is general secretary of the National Council of Churches. I had interviewed her before and been struck by her candor, so she made a perfect representative of the Mainline Protestant churches.

I wanted to interview someone from the Pentecostal tradition, so I called the Assemblies of God, the largest Pentecostal church in the United States; they suggested Sandra Clopine, head of the church's education department. Sandra, an ordained minister, is also head of the National Association of Evangelicals' women's division.

After two prominent Evangelicals canceled out at the last minute, Tim Jones at *Christianity Today* suggested that I interview Richard Foster. When I stumbled across an interview with Foster in *U.S. Catholic* just a few hours later, I didn't need any further convincing. Foster, a Quaker, has worked on prayer with Christians from many traditions.

I worked with George Gallup, Jr., writing two books and five years' worth of columns, and I knew of his involvement in prayer groups. That was a perspective I wanted, so I asked George to take part. George, an Episcopalian with strong Evangelical overtones, has also done some unique research on the impact of prayer.

I asked Church Women United to recommend several prominent church women and chose their president, Ann Garvin, an active community volunteer and a member of the African Methodist Episcopal Church.

John Borelli, who runs the U.S. Catholic Conference office dealing with religions outside of Christianity and Judaism, recommended Rajshri Gopal as a Hindu who could successfully articulate her beliefs.

Billy Graham was an obvious choice for this book. He's cutting back his schedule because of age and illness, but Mary Becker of his staff provided me with quotes taken from his speeches and public interviews. I worked them into a narrative, and Graham himself made some changes and additions.

Andrew Greeley—priest, sociologist, and novelist—was a natural subject. He prays and also studies people who do.

High Star is a Lakota Sioux "singer," or medicine man. Sami Toinetta, a Lakota who works for the National Council of Churches, referred me to him, as he is her spiritual adviser.

Two longtime friends, Rabbi Jim Rudin, of the American Jewish Committee, and Rabbi David Saperstein, of the Union of American Hebrew Congregations, both said that if I wanted to talk to someone who really knew Jewish prayer, I should talk to Rabbi Larry Kushner in Boston. So I did.

I've known Norman Lear for more than a decade; for part of that time I worked with him at People for the American Way. While many people view Norman as completely secular in outlook, I knew him as a man who had a deeply spiritual nature that was not tied to any one religious tradition. He was another natural to include, proof that those with no religious affiliation still have a spiritual dimension.

I've long admired Congressman John Lewis of Georgia, a veteran civil rights leader, and was struck by a recent comment by Georgia governor Zell Miller, who said that many people today regard Lewis as a saint.

Martin Marty, arguably the most quoted person in American religion, was another natural choice. A church historian, Lutheran minister, and all-around expert on religion, Martin has never given a bad interview; the one he gave me was exceptional.

Carol Mu'min, a black Muslim active in interfaith activities, came at the recommendation of Clark Lobenstine, director of the Interfaith Conference of Greater Washington.

Finding a Buddhist to interview for this book was difficult because I frequently ran into the objection "Buddhists don't pray." They may not pray, but they do prayerlike things in a spiritual way. When Ronald Nakasone's name turned up twice—recommended by Kathy Nolan, herself a Buddhist; and by the Institute for Buddhist Studies at Berkeley, recommended by Joan Connell—I took it as a sign and got an excellent interview from Ron.

I first interviewed Marlene Payne, a Mormon and a psychiatrist, twelve years ago during the controversy over Sonia Johnson, a feminist Mormon. Marlene helped me overcome some preconceptions about Mormons; she also helped me understand that both feminists and Mormon women were under great pressure to "have it all," even if they differed about what the "all" means. I thought Marlene would be thoughtful on prayer, and I was right.

I worked on a project with Jane Redmont, a Catholic

writer, several years ago and thought of her as someone with a strong social-justice and feminist perspective.

I asked Ron Cruz, who heads the U.S. Catholic Conference office for Hispanic Affairs, to recommend a grassroots Hispanic Catholic, and he urged me to talk to Mary Frances Robles, the daughter of a close family friend.

When I told Jim Rudin that I wanted to talk to a young Jewish person about prayer, he suggested that I talk with his daughter, Eve; once again I took his advice.

Many people I spoke with urged me to interview Robert Schuller, and I was glad to do so. His comments were short, but pithy. Schuller, a member of the Dutch Reformed Church, prides himself on being a Mainline Protestant television preacher.

Brad Pokorny, of the Baha'i International office in New York, put me in touch with Dan Seals; a fan of Dan's country and pop music, I was delighted to interview him.

I asked the Reverend Leonid Kishkovsky, former president of the National Council of Churches and a leader of the Orthodox Church in America, to recommend a member of his church; he led me to Eleana Silk, a librarian at Saint Vladimir's Seminary, whose interest in oral history heightened her interest in this project.

My first choice for a prominent Catholic bishop was Archbishop Rembert Weakland, of Milwaukee. His candor has made him unpopular at the Vatican, but he is a hero to a large number of American Catholics. He's also a Benedictine monk who knows a great deal about prayer.

At one point I told Jane Redmont about how difficult it was to put together the right demographic mix for this book. I said I needed a young professional woman with a family who belonged to a Mainline Protestant

church. She said I'd just described Lisa Wood, an Episcopalian.

To begin each interview, I developed a set of base
questions and I added other questions as they seemed appropriate for each subject. These are the questions I
asked each subject:

How do you define prayer?

To whom do you pray?

When did prayer first become important to you?

How has prayer changed for you?

How do you pray?

Do you make up your prayers as you pray, or do you
use any standard prayers?

Do you use different types of prayers at different times?

Do you have a favorite prayer?

Have you had some particularly meaningful prayer experiences?

How long do you pray?

How often do you pray?

Do you pray silently or out loud?

Do you meditate?

When you pray, do you ask for things? Guidance?
Blessings? Forgiveness?

What happens to you during prayer? What about afterward?

Does prayer give you a sense of peace?

Does God "talk" to you?

Do you feel God's presence?

Do you get answers to your prayers?

When and how do you pray with others? In large or
small groups? Do you use a liturgy?

How does your prayer affect your relationships with
other people?

How does your prayer affect your work?

How does your prayer relate to the broader community? Society? Social justice?

Not everyone answered every question, and some responses prompted many other questions. But this list proved to be a valuable tool in prompting more than two dozen fascinating glimpses of Americans at prayer. You might want to sit down and ask yourself the questions from this list; they may help you to consider and understand the significance of prayer in your own life.

PHILIP C. BOM

Philip C. Bom is a professor in the School of Public Policy at Regent University in Virginia Beach, and the author of Academocracy *(1976) and* Trudeau's Canada *(1977). He is an elder in the Presbyterian Church of America, which was formed in the 1970s to counter what its members saw as liberalism in the southern Presbyterian church. Bom is married and has three children.*

Prayer is a direct communion between the Creator, God, and the creature, man. Man is made in the image of God to pray and to work, and to seek the Father's will in both (just as Jesus did). Prayer also includes petition—that is, asking God to intercede in the lives of people and nations.

I pray to God the Father, the Maker of Heaven and earth, and to Jesus Christ, my Savior and Redeemer of mankind. When I talk about thanking Him for the seasons, for the springtime, I direct my thoughts more to God the Father as Creator. When it comes to the salvation of myself and my family, I direct my thoughts much more to Jesus as my Savior.

I was brought up in a Christian home where prayer was an integral part of family devotion. As a child I understood my parents' trust in God the Father; I knew that He would provide for our needs and guide us in our daily walk.

In the past I may have prayed absentmindedly or repetitiously or out of mere habit. Prayer is a spiritual activity, but it can still be a selfish action. Now it has become for me a discipline of the heart and mind. I work on my prayer to refine my communion with God so that I can concentrate on glorifying God and not remain focused on my own needs and desires. Prayer has made my walk with the Lord much more personal and intimate.

I pray with my eyes closed, usually sitting down, before and after reading Scripture. Depending on the occasion, my prayers last from one to fifteen minutes. My wife and I pray together each morning and evening. Our personal, private prayers are spontaneous, reflecting Scripture readings and current needs among family, friends, church, and the world. On special occasions, such as national holidays and holy days, I may use the Episcopal Book of Common Prayer or a Catholic prayer book.

Next to the Lord's Prayer I love the prayer ascribed to Saint Francis of Assisi, especially the first line:

Lord, make me an instrument of your peace.
  Where there is hatred, let me sow love,
  Where there is injury, pardon;
  Where there is doubt, faith;
  Where there is despair, hope;
  Where there is darkness, light;
  And where there is sadness, joy.

O, divine Master, grant that I may not so much
  seek to be consoled as to console,
  to be understood as to understand,
  to be loved, as to love.

Because it is in giving that we receive,
  it is in pardoning that we are pardoned,
  and it is in dying that we are born to eternal life.

In addition to morning and evening prayers I pray before meals and at the beginning of my classes. Of course at any time during the day, I may respond to a special need with a short prayer.

When I pray, I specifically ask for wisdom, blessing (contentment), guidance, and direction in my personal and professional life. I ask not from a "want list" but in the knowledge of my dependence upon God and Father. I ask in the certainty that He will answer (in)directly in His way and in His timing. I am afraid of asking "amiss" (James 4:3), using God for my pet projects or priorities.

The "wedding text" my wife and I chose was Matthew 6:33—"But seek ye first the kingdom of God, and his righteousness; and all these things shall be added unto you"—and that is what we have tried to do with many failures. God has blessed us with a diversity of professional opportunities and with many answers to prayers relating to family members. However, when we lost our son, we found that God does not always answer in the way we request.

During prayer I transcend time and place. I experience the communion of the saints, globally and locally. I can almost visualize family and friends. Although not present physically, I am with them spiritually, through my imagination. The prayer becomes so intense that the distance between us disappears, and it becomes very much an intimate prayer. When I pray for friends in China, I envision them, and pray for their favor, blessing, and protection.

When I pray for those who are persecuted, for my fellow believers in what used to be the USSR or in China, I pray intensely, so that I know the experience of their deprivation of religious freedom. I've read enough books about what it means to be imprisoned, to be persecuted, so I can sense their deprivation and persecution. I find it so amazing that even though you're far away physically, spiritually you're very near. It's very personal, very intimate.

After such intercessory prayer I experience peace, for God will provide for their needs and protection. Prayer gives me a sense of peace. It enables me to accept that "whatever my God ordains is right."

God has heard both major and minor petitions that my wife and I have made. Over the years our family has traveled hundreds of thousands of miles by car, so we have always prayed for safety. Our prayers for traveling mercies have been answered, even to the extent that we suffered no injuries when a major accident happened. Another time we were traveling along the interstate at night when a car suddenly drove toward us on our side of the road. Once again God fully protected us.

Through prayer my relationship with others is enriched. Friendships deepen, for prayer enables people to experience communion. If I encounter relational problems with others, I pray for them, which enables me to forgive them and see problems in a broader and less personal context. At church I lead the congregation in prayer about once a month and also share in smaller prayer groups. I find that praying with and for colleagues and students deepens relationships.

When our twenty-two-year-old son died unexpectedly, my wife and I experienced remarkable peace and comfort in answer to the many prayers of family and friends. During the first ten hours after we had heard the terrible news, we were dazed and in shock. At noon we knew that hundreds would hear of our loss at the university chapel service and would start praying. My wife and I sat on the sofa to rest and to receive whatever strength the Lord could provide during the intercessory prayer. Slowly we could feel our shock and turmoil slip away, to be replaced by an abiding peace and comfort. It truly was amazing! Our hearts and minds were filled with a quietude of spirit and an assurance of God's presence. An immediate answer to prayer! That peace "beyond understanding" has remained with us in the six years since our son's death.

Prayer with students restores and enriches the idea of University, an intimate relationship between teacher (senior scholar) and students (junior scholars). Together we seek God's truth, rather than the professor's way of intellectual arrogance. I pray before each class with the students for wisdom, understanding, and peace in the world. I pray that my professional work may be a form of worship in which I seek God's truth and purpose and speak "truth to power." Prayer gives meaning and direction to my work. It provides me with a purpose for scholarship: to transform hearts and minds. Prayer helps me to desire knowledge, but not for the sake of knowledge (intellectualism).

No, knowledge is there to shape the character of students and society. It is my heart's desire to develop a Christian mind and to live a God-centered life of learning and discerning. Such a Christian mind seeks to integrate (Christian) philosophy and public policy. I now see politics as a ministry of justice rather than as a power game. For me a model prayer life of a public official is that of Daniel (sixth century B.C.) who served as "prime minister" under the Persian emperor Darius. Even though he was under tremendous pressure and persecution, he kept up his habit of praying three times a day for political wisdom. We read that in conducting his governmental affairs "he was trustworthy and neither corrupt nor negligent" (Dan. 6:4). What an example for our own public officials!

Recently I participated in a community prayer meeting in which I led a prayer for the world. We prayed for harmony in industrial relations, for domestic tranquillity in the city and state, for peace and righteousness both in our nation and in the world. One of my favorite prayers for the nation is by Josiah Gilbert Holland, with the first two lines being of particular relevance:

God, give us Men! A time like this demands
Strong minds, great hearts, true faith and ready hands.
　　Men whom the lust of office does not kill;
Men whom the spoils of office cannot buy;
　　Men who possess opinions and a will;
Men who have honor; men who will not lie;
Men who can stand before a demagogue
　　And damn his treacherous flatteries without winking!
Tall men, sun-crowned, who live above the fog
　　In public duty and in private thinking;
For while the rabble, with their thumb-worn creeds,
Their large professions and their little deeds,
Mingle in selfish strife, lo! Freedom weeps,
Wrong rules the land and waiting Justice sleeps.

SIDNEY CALLAHAN

Sidney Callahan, a Catholic, is an author, psychologist, lecturer, and a professor at Mercy College in Dobbs Ferry, New York. Her books include Parents Forever: You and Your Adult Children *(1992);* In Good Conscience: Reason and Emotion in Moral Decisionmaking *(1991);* With All Our Heart and Mind: The Spiritual Works of Mercy in a Psychological Age *(1988); and* Abortion: Understanding Differences *(1984). She is married to Daniel Callahan, with whom she has six grown children.*

Prayer for me is always addressed to God, and it expresses the traditional definition of "lifting the mind and heart to God." But because I have never been able to master a disciplined life in the way that all the spiritual manuals discuss as the first thing you must do, I've never been able to set aside time to pray in an organized way. I do depend very much on always going to church on Sundays and being very punctilious in fulfilling all the obligations of the church. Going to Mass and worship at Mass is my one grip on structure—especially in my own parish church, where I can be less self-conscious. I am never happy at big conferences where they have ritzy-ditzy, super-duper kinds of liturgies; I don't like them. I'm made too self-conscious there and can't lose myself in prayer or devotions. I like my own ordinary church, my own place on the rear right aisle, where I am unself-consciously able to follow the Mass and be a part of it.

So the liturgy is very important to me because that's my one structural anchor for prayer.

But that isn't all. In my own disorganized way I pray all the time during the day and in all kinds of situations. Little things cue you in to prayer during the day—even going to the bathroom. It may not seem very elegant, but anytime we are self-conscious and turned in upon ourselves is a time when we can lift ourselves up to God. And certainly during orgasm is a wonderful moment of prayer—it's a time of ecstasy, a wonderful gift of physical delight. When I used to nurse babies, that, too, was a natural time to pray. Even in the middle of a wonderful dinner party, when everyone's having a wonderful time and eating food, that's a moment when you can pray.

I learned to pray two or three Marian prayers. I converted in 1953, so I did not have proper schooling in these things and did not learn things by heart. But I have a great devotion to Mary. I think Marian devotion is one of the particular gifts of the Catholic church. I took Mary as my baptismal name, realizing that that was an affirmation of all the things Catholic you can get that you don't get in the Protestant religion: the incarnational, the liturgical, what I now recognize as the "feminine" aspects of Catholicism. Recently I learned Marian prayers, but because I have such a hard time learning things by heart, I have to say them all the time to keep remembering them. I pray the Angelus, the traditional prayer that was said three times a day in the French countryside. We happen to have a convent nearby; a bell there is rung three times a day, and this reminds me to pray. The Angelus is a Marian prayer, when you say the Hail Mary three times as a refrain. It goes like this: "An Angel of the Lord declared unto Mary and she conceived of the Holy Ghost . . . Hail Mary . . . Behold the Handmaiden of the Lord . . . Be it done unto me according to Thy Word . . . Hail Mary."

Then I do "Hail, Holy Queen" because I think that's such a lovely prayer:

Hail Holy Queen
Mother of Mercy, Our Life, Our Sweetness and Our Hope
To thee do we cry poor banished children of Eve,
To thee do we send up our sighs.
Mourning and weeping in this Valley of Tears.
Turn then most gracious advocate
Thine eyes of mercy toward us.
And after this our exile
Show unto us the blessed fruit of thy womb Jesus
O clement, o loving o sweet Virgin Mary
Pray for us o Holy Mother of God
That we may be made worthy of the promises of Christ.

I might say these prayers when I'm running, or in the health club in the steam room. The latter is a wonderful place to pray. I thought it was unique to me—it just seemed so appropriate to be praying while you're sitting there sweating and steaming—but it turns out that the American Indians used sweat lodges to pray, so there's never anything unusual and new. You always find that somebody else has done these things before you. Well, maybe while driving—*that* must be perfectly modern; people in the past couldn't have done that!

The Marian prayers are not the only thing I pray. I pray about everything. It just comes to me; I say things or discuss things or pray for somebody or try to come to some conclusion about something if I have a problem. I've gotten incredible answers to prayer, and it makes me wonder why I don't pray more since I've always been answered and so many wonderful things have come my way.

Apparently there are two ways of devotion. There is

the negative way, where you strip away everything. That way is very Buddhist; you become much more detached, and God is seen in the nothingness. But there's another approach, which goes to God through things, through happiness, through people, through experiences, through the sensual, physical, social world. That's definitely my approach.

I ask for everything—everything I need. My children and my family are my personal, private objects of prayer. Of course I occasionally pray for peace and public causes. But I feel the liturgy is where I do my public praying, and I use my private praying for my husband and children and friends whom I know are in need or have problems.

Then I pray for guidance. For example, what should I write my next book about? I know I'm going to spend four years on it, so what is the right thing to write about? Should I go back to doing therapy or stay in teaching? If I have a problem of conscience—that is, what is the right thing to do in some situation—I pray about that. As a scientifically minded person or a psychologist, I'm always worried about self-deception and whether my own perceptions are the correct perceptions or not. Since you always know you can be self-deceived, I mull it over a long time and listen to intuitions that come, some of them very slowly, some of them out of the blue. I think about them critically and ask if these are the real voice of God or not. "Discernment of spirits" is a very ancient and subtle kind of activity, and I consider it a real act of prudence to sift through all these things and see how they relate to everything else I know. I let it settle awhile, and then usually, slowly, some sense of confidence will come out of that and I will feel that this is the answer.

Prayer always makes me feel wonderful because it

makes me feel more alive, or more spirited, or more happy, or more energized, or more peaceful. It immediately opens up the world to me. I've never had that "dark night of the soul" or "God is absent" feeling. That's probably because I'm a fragile plant and need a lot of water; God is guiding me in this very, very, easygoing, positive way, because I couldn't take it if I had to have one of those long times of doubt or dryness. But my temperament is a happy one in certain ways—almost an emotional, ecstatic consciousness. Since as a psychologist I'm aware of manic disorders of euphoria, I used to worry about my temperament all the time. But then I thought, "We're all supposed to be different, and this is just my way." As you get older, you think, "This is just my temperament, and this is the way it is. I'm not going to try to be some other way. It wouldn't be me."

I do pray all the time about my work. Before I go in and teach or give a talk, I think, "Please use me in the right way." If I'm writing, I try to dedicate the experience to God; I offer it up at the beginning or ask for good advice or inspiration. I even pray to get myself *to* work! I'm a very lazy person; I love just to lie around and have fun and read or chat or enjoy life. If I have a hundred exams to grade or a deadline due, I pray to do it and not just procrastinate!

Of course when you're actually completely working, you can't be thinking about anything else except what you're doing. I've never understood the people who say they feel the constant presence of God even when they're struggling to get this particular paragraph in shape. I think you lose yourself; your attention goes to whatever it is that you have to do. That's complete, total absorption in a task. So what I do is offer my work up before I start and hope that it's been received, but it seems to me that what I'm supposed to be doing is be totally and completely absorbed and focused on my task. I'm sure that that's one of the reasons why ascetics and church fathers and many people in the past were so suspicious of sexuality; it is an absorbing, altered state of consciousness, just like complete and intense work. You can't pray while you're doing that, and so they felt it was suspect.

If I have trouble with somebody or get into a conflict, I always pray about it. And if I feel that other people, like my children or my family, are having difficulty in development or in any kind of way—if they're sick or looking for jobs or can't seem to get themselves together or a certain loving relationship goes bad for them—I pray about that. No one in my family is an active believer at present, so I pray for them to come back to God. I'm grateful, too, when I pray. If you ask what my prayer is about, it mostly consists of "Help!" and "Thank you!" . . . although you can't help but pay more attention to the things you think are going wrong. Yes, you want to be thankful for certain things, but usually you will pray for things that have gone wrong.

I pray to stop being selfish. I could live by myself and be happy, but that seems to me to be totally a temptation and wrong. I pray to make myself give more money away and work more in my causes. I am committed to a lot of causes that are unpopular: peace and pro-life. All my friends and everybody I know is pro-choice, and it's hard for me to engage in social conflict. So I pray to help myself overcome lethargy, inertia, self-complacency, and to make myself turn outward.

One of the things I'm sorry about is that I've never had a spiritual director or anyone like that. It's probably part of my disorganization, or free-flow approach. If I really want to grow spiritually, my next step is to get a spiritual director. I do believe in counseling and consulting with one's friends, although interestingly enough, I don't really talk to anyone about prayer.

I believe that all kinds of people have mystical experiences but don't talk about them because other people will think they're crazy. I have had feminine images of God, feelings that God was with me, or that the Virgin Mary appeared and told me I would be well from an illness I had. (It took two years, but eventually I was totally cured.) But being a psychologist, I'm also always skeptical, so I wonder if perhaps these images I've seen are just some form of semihallucination. I'm interested in someday writing about this, about women who hear voices—Joan of Arc and all of that. Or maybe it's just my nature in particular that makes it easy for me to have religious experiences of great joy and be easily moved to tears.

JOAN BROWN CAMPBELL

The Reverend Joan Brown Campbell is general secretary of the National Council of Churches (NCC). She is an ordained minister in both the Christian Church (Disciples of Christ) and the American Baptist Churches, and is the first woman to serve as NCC general secretary. She has been closely associated with the NCC for more than twenty years and was previously associate director of the Greater Cleveland Interchurch Council and pastor of Euclid Baptist Church in Cleveland. Campbell has three grown children and four grandchildren, and is a member and elder of the Park Avenue Christian Church in New York City.

I think of prayer as a conversation with God. For me it's a deeply spiritual experience. Prayer is always trusting; you open yourself to an immediate intimacy in your relationship to God. I'm a Disciple, and Disciples don't have written prayer books. What is very much part of the Disciple tradition is to pray from the mind and heart.

Prayer is so much a part of my daily life. On occasion I will have an actual conscious time of prayer. But I also realize that many times during the day I will say, almost out loud, "Dear God, take this from me." In my job there are a lot of unsolvable problems. So I will sometimes say to myself, "Dear God, take this, work with this, for I don't know what the answers are; help me to know." And there is a lot of prayer in my life that is much more a kind of conversation that is frequent and often at times of joy. I'm very conscious of my years with the black church, where people say a deep-felt "Thank you, Jesus" when something good happens. When something happens that has a sort of profound human quality to it, I will find myself saying, "Thank you, Jesus." And I will often pray because I have so much writing to do. To achieve inspiration, I sometimes realize that I am almost in a state of prayer. In fact the writing of a sermon itself is almost a prayer. It's not an academic exercise, but more of a prayer time when you are searching for the inspiration. I feel writing sermons is really a major responsibility, for you are working with the word of God.

Every day I have a kind of disciplined time when I read from the Scripture. And every year at Lent I use a little book put out by the Consultation on Church Union called *Liberation and Unity*, written largely by black church leaders. I have a particular lack of information about the Orthodox churches, so this year I've used a couple of prayer guides that our Orthodox staff have given me. I also use their Holy Week guide. Because I'm out so much speaking on a Sunday, I have very little congregational life of my own. It's the first time in my life I have not had real roots in a congregation, so I follow the lectionary for my own edification. During the week I will sometimes read the lessons that are part of the lectionary because it keeps me in touch with what the Scriptures would be if I were regularly in a congregation; the lectionary takes me through the church year. Oh, and I also use the Episcopal Prayer Book a lot; I'm very, very fond of it. It is their gift to all of us. I have many times in which I must pray publicly, and for those times when I'm without inspiration for a public prayer, the Episcopal Prayer Book never fails to be helpful.

My prayer life has changed over the years. When I was younger, I sometimes felt my prayers were not answered because, in a way, I did not have enough life experience to know what it meant for them to *be* answered. God never answers our prayers in a direct way; cause-and-effect are not immediate in prayer. Now as I look back over my life, I can say that my prayers *have* been answered. One of my prayers has always been that I might have a meaningful life, that I might have a full life, that I might be given things to do that make a difference. My father, when I was a child, was always saying, "Much has been given you, much will be required of you." I remember that being said to me over and over again. I suppose the psychiatrists wouldn't like that so much today, but in fact it was for me a constant thing I heard as a child, and it was not negative. *You've been given a lot of gifts, and much is going to be required of you.* Because of that I would always pray that I would find work to do and a life to lead that was worthy of what I had been given.

As I look back over my life, I see the way in which my prayers have been answered, although it's not the way I would have designed it. But they do weave something of a tapestry that makes sense. And I think once you get older, you say, "Thank God that I *wasn't* allowed to design it." I have a much better life for having been guided than if I had myself been able, every step of the way, to do what I thought was the right thing to do. But I only know that in looking back. My father died very young, and I remember praying that he would live. I see now that that was not to be. At the time, though, it feels very much as though your immediate prayer is not answered. So we need to remember something else my father told me. Once after I prayed for something that didn't happen, he said, "Well, this is not the purpose. You don't pray so that you get something, you pray so that you *receive* something—but it's not the immediate thing that you ask for." I have found myself straining to accept that. There are times when I don't want to add to my prayer,

"Your will be done," because I really want it my way. And that's pretty normal. But I've certainly learned in my life that God's way is not always my way, and thank goodness it isn't. Still, it's usually in retrospect that you believe and accept this.

I think we do pray our deepest, most profound prayers when much is at risk; it's not an accident that we're very close to God in times of trouble. I have said sometimes in sermons that it's no accident that Jesus prayed in the face of the cross. We pray our "Jesus deepest" prayers and our most heartfelt prayers when we are facing imminent danger. You pray when you feel vulnerable and when you need more than you can bring to a situation. In this job I feel that all the time. In a sense it's such an undoable job that I find myself often saying, "God, this is not doable, help me to see the way through some of this." I think a way is made. You can get discouraged doing ecumenical work because it's very slow and without a lot of rewards. But I've never become desperate or felt like giving up, and that is very much because of my own prayer life. I feel very much that God will be ready for us, and we can tap into that power. What's there pulls us that way. It doesn't matter what we do or don't do, unity is going to come. I couldn't have done this work for thirty years or more if I didn't have some feeling that unity of all life was God's will for this world.

So God is, for me, very much a source of strength and power. There are days when I literally think that I would not get through the day if I didn't have a feeling that I could pray and be heard. It isn't even about receiving an answer, it's about *knowing* that there's a force there. For me it's much more a sense of power-for-good than it is of seeing a person.

I have absolutely felt God's presence when I prayed, but I don't have an image of God in my mind. People always ask me that as a woman: "Do you think of God as male or female?" and I never really do. I don't call up an image. I do feel a sense of power; there's a presence I can feel. But I've never been so comfortable with the paintings of Jesus that we have, so I never call them up in my mind.

I often think about my father when I pray. He was a doctor and he was very, very rarely at home. But he always was there at night, and he was the one—for reasons I don't even know, now—who would sit with us at night. During the Second World War—I was probably six or seven years old when the war began, maybe older—people got into the conflict gradually. It didn't start with everybody. So my father and I would first pray for the Italians and the Ethiopians. Then I can remember when we added the Germans and the French and the Japanese. My prayer time was sort of like my lesson in world history. Always my father said, "You must pray for both sides; you can't pray for just our side." But the list got very long as more and more countries got involved, and so finally one night he said, "Let's just pray for the Allies and the Axis."

My father taught me so much about prayer. I was not a very big kid when he said, "Let me tell you about prayer. If you're on the railroad track, and you are tied down, and the train is coming, pray to God that that train will stop. If you are on the railroad track and you are not tied down, don't pray to God; get up and move off the track if the train is coming." That lesson has stayed in my mind. *Don't bother God with things you're expected to do with your own human intelligence.* What it results in for me is that prayer comes up at times when I feel that I've used what I've been given and there needs to be a little help beyond what I have to offer.

I was very sick once with a heart attack, and prayer in

such times affects your relationship to God. I was one of those who was technically dead for seconds. I remember waking up and having everybody around my bed. Many people say that once you go through that, you are never again afraid of death. Yet there's a lot you *would* miss; I think you give up life only with very great difficulty. There are children and grandchildren and tasks that have to be completed. Those are things that give you life. But having really faced death made me realize I wasn't afraid of it.

I've spent most of my life on social justice. Many, many of my public prayers—and that doesn't mean that they're not also personal prayers—have been related to the issues of justice and peace, particularly to the issue of race. I found myself, even this morning, thinking about the people in Los Angeles (awaiting the verdict in the second Rodney King trial) and praying that God will provide peace in that city and see that justice is done. I pray for Bill Clinton, because I think he's trying to bring justice to a land where there's been terrific miscarriages of justice. I've been to the Middle East, and I pray for all of them there. You don't forget the people in the Middle East once you've been there and seen their situation. I worked with Martin Luther King, so a lot of my prayers are related to social justice. For me social issues are also personal issues. I don't separate them one from the other.

I think prayer is as important as life itself. I pray for the people around me, for my family in times of sadness or joy. I am invested in teaching my grandchildren to pray—not that their parents aren't also—but I would be very sad if my grandchildren didn't have some knowledge of God and that prayer wasn't part of their lives. I have not had such an easy life, but it's prayer that's made up for it. As I think about it, I'm a little teary; prayer has been in my life a very real source of strength. God is not indifferent. God is close and intimate. I covet that for everyone, but especially for my grandchildren, where my personal prayer and my special love converge. I guess I believe that prayer is the natural language of love.

SANDRA GOODWIN CLOPINE

Sandra Goodwin Clopine, a former missionary, is Coordinator for the National Prayer Center of the Assemblies of God in Springfield, Missouri. She is also chair of the Women's Commission of the National Association of Evangelicals. She is a member of Delta Epsilon Chi, the honor society for the American Association of Bible Colleges, and is secretary of the North American chapter of the International Pentecostal Press Association. She and her husband, Myron, have five children and fourteen grandchildren.

Prayer is intimate communication with the Lord. To put it in very simple terms, it's just talking with the Lord; we don't need to use high-sounding words or try to structure our sentences to impress anybody. I like to think of the Lord as sitting in a chair near me and I am conversing with Him.

To me the purpose of praying is to move the pray-er into God's perspective. Theologian John Huess said that prayer was more a matter of clearing away the underbrush to get a view than it was of making a list of demands. I really feel that way. I think the more time we spend in prayer, the more we begin to see things from God's perspective. By God's perspective I mean that He has the whole view of everything and we see it from one little time frame. I believe that as He sees the whole picture, He knows what is best in each situation. We can't always see it that way, but I think that as we pray, He helps us see more clearly. What we cannot see He helps us accept.

Prayer involves the reading of God's word. I usually like to have the Bible near me, either to read something before I pray or when I feel directed toward a certain passage. Prayer is a two-way communication. Not only do we speak to our Heavenly Father, but He speaks to us. Prayer involves submitting ourselves to God and presenting our requests to Him. As we listen for instruction, we then thank Him for allowing us to be used in some way to help meet the need. We don't assume that God is going to "zap" us with an answer. Rather He will reveal to us ways we can be a part of the answer.

I have different ways of praying. My devotional time in the morning is different from my more structured prayers, when I focus on various aspects of society, my community, my family, and more personal needs, such as the work that I do. For instance on Sunday my prayer focuses on ministry to the Lord: my church's services and pastoral staff, my family's involvement in church, my personal relationship with the Lord, and my expectations for meeting Him in His house. As an ordained minister I pray for ministries the Lord has opened to me. Most of the time I use spontaneous prayers, or at times I read prayers from the Bible. Sometimes I feel impressed to write a prayer, it's as if I am writing a letter to the Lord.

Mondays my prayer focus is about my work needs, our schools, and those who teach our nation's children. Tuesdays I pray about ministry to women. Our denominational women's organization has a day-of-prayer emphasis on Tuesdays for the more than 400,000 women and girls involved. We pray for leadership at all levels and for issues women are burdened with, such as abortion, pornography, family abuse, AIDS, the breakup of the home, and many others.

Each Wednesday my focus is on national, state, and local government. I pray for legislators, pending legislation, economic conditions, and current events. Scripture admonishes us to pray "for kings and all those in authority, that we may live peaceful and quiet lives in all godliness and holiness" (1 Tim. 2:2, NIV).

Thursdays are structured for praying about winning the world to Christ. I pray for foreign missionaries, Bible schools around the world, and governments that hinder the spread of the Gospel. On Fridays I pray for my own denomination, its executive leaders, pastors and congregations, and departmental programs for children, youth, and adults. On Saturdays my prayer focus is Mission America: home missionaries, intercultural ministries, inner cities, ministries on our college campuses, ministries to people of various addictions, new churches that are being established, and my own neighbors.

My morning devotional time, which averages about fifteen minutes each day, is a time in which I do not use a notebook. During my longer, more structured prayers I often use a simple spiral notebook to write down things that come to mind while I pray. People's names may come to my mind and I like to make note of them, for I feel those people may need special prayer. I also like to write down those Scriptures that come to mind. Later I can go back and be reminded of what I felt at the time of prayer. I also may write a couple of lines, or sometimes a whole page, about my feelings at the time.

In my devotional time each morning I like to use what I call the ABCs of prayer:

A. Adore Him for who He is. In other words, worship Him as God Almighty rather than come to Him with a big list of wants.

B. Believe Him for what He says. Have faith in His word.

C. Confess my need of all He has; commit my will to His.

Sometimes I read one of my favorite prayers, the Lord's Prayer or the prayer in Saint John, chapter 17. I also read other prayers, such as the prayer of Saint Francis of Assisi.

Besides my morning devotional time I pray at other times throughout the day. For example I have on my desk at work the birthdates of our church women's leaders across the nation. I pray for them from time to time. There are times while driving the car that I ask for the Lord's protection or pray for something that comes to my mind during the day. For me it is not a matter of going somewhere to kneel and pray but of just being impressed with something and praying at that very moment.

As a Pentecostal I sometimes pray out loud. I don't mean with a screaming voice, but just talking to the Lord, focusing on the Lord Himself. Many times it is more appropriate to pray silently. In our church services the corporate body often prays together. That can be done with one person leading and others standing in agreement with the prayer being prayed. Sometimes we are asked to break into groups of four to six and each share a request. We will either all pray together about that request or one by one. This may be done silently or it may be done by all of us together praying out loud. We feel it is helpful to personalize each need that is presented. I have been involved in what we call Prayer Walks, where we walk around a certain area or building with another person and pray in conversational tones as though we are talking with each other; actually we are talking to the Lord.

Often I pray with other people. We have a prayer meeting in our home about once a month for people in our subdivision. Usually that involves praying with families about special needs in their homes and in our community. My husband and I pray and read the Bible together each day, and we usually pray with guests who come to our home to visit. Before they leave, we join hands and offer a short prayer. We also attend prayer meetings at our church.

In my private prayer time I sometimes pray in tongues. It's very uplifting and builds me up in my faith, as the Scripture indicates in the Book of Jude, verse 20: "But you, dear friends, build yourselves up in your most holy faith and pray in the Holy Spirit." I feel I am drawn closer to the Lord in those times. Other times I feel a special heaviness on my heart, a burden for somebody or some situation. Many times I do not know what the situation is, and without planning to do so I begin praying in tongues. When we don't know what the problem is, the Bible tells us that the Spirit knows and prays through us: "We do not know what we ought to pray for, but the Spirit himself intercedes for us with groans that words cannot express" (Rom. 8:26, NIV). After praying I feel a great satisfaction in my heart that the Lord has met the need in the way that He sees it even though I may not even know the details. Those prayers seem to have a special unction, an added dimension through which the Lord ministers to me, the pray-er, and to the one(s) for whom I am praying.

Prayer gives me a sense of peace even when I am in the midst of turmoil or something I cannot understand. At the conclusion of prayer I feel a peace in my heart, knowing that God has it all in His control. I have had those times when I have been completely overwhelmed in prayer by the simple fact that I was in the presence of the King of Kings and Lord of Lords. I have been humbled by the fact that a human being can approach the

God that created the Universe, the God of total perfection. Sometimes I have been so completely overwhelmed that I find myself weeping, not even able to form words, and have prostrated myself on the floor with a sense of total unworthiness. I have never seen lights flashing, and never heard an audible voice speaking to me at those times, but they have been stamped on my heart as times that God met me in a very significant way.

Growing up, I knew only a little about prayer, but the two prayer meetings each week in my home church really helped establish me in the Lord and in prayer. Up until that time all I knew about prayer was that if you were in a very desperate circumstance, you could cry out to God, "Help me!" Later I learned that prayer was such a privilege and that as I prayed, I wanted to do more praying. I found that the Lord was a friend whom I wanted to be with often, and that strengthened my prayer life. And I learned that prayer was much more than a list of requests. Prayer has become a time of real enjoyment and personal fulfillment. When I was widowed at the age of twenty-six, I learned that prayer was not something I had to go someplace to do; there was an intimacy with the Lord so that anytime, day or night, I could look up to Him with a prayer for forgiveness or whatever else I felt at the particular moment. This kind of spontaneous, unplanned prayer has become a pattern of my life, and I have enjoyed it so much since then.

The newspaper and the TV news are real good sources of information to help us pray. Families can use some of those terrible news tragedies as opportunities to gather their children together and say, "Let's pray about what we've just seen (or read); let's pray for those people in that foreign country or city far away. Let's pray about some of the decisions being made in Washington, D.C. Let's pray about what's happening in Congress."

In speaking to others and in helping myself concerning prayer, I have used these three facts to keep on target:

1. Make a decision and share it. In other words let someone know you intend to pray today. My husband knows of my early-morning prayer time and helps me have that time available for prayer.

2. Make an appointment and keep it. Find a time that suits your schedule and be faithful to it each day. It may be early morning, it may be late at night, or it may be during the children's nap time. The time you choose is not important. The important thing is meeting God.

3. Make an expression and write it. You should keep fresh in your mind the things you were impressed with during your prayer time. I look back over prayer notebooks and find things long forgotten are great blessings today.

I feel that I have had some very definite answers to prayer. For instance when I was on the mission field, there were situations that held danger. At those times I prayed, and the Lord gave me His peace. He saw me through some situations that were pretty hectic. I have a personal feeling, however, that God answers *every* prayer, even though He may not do it the very way I have it programmed in my mind. Sometimes the answer may be "Not now." I may look back a month from now and see that God did answer the prayer I prayed, but maybe not exactly the way I had it planned. He did, however, through time, work it out, and only now can I see that His way was best. Or sometimes the answer may be a definite no. At the time it may be very difficult for us to see it as no. Yet we can go away from that prayer time having placed the request in God's hands and letting Him be in control of it.

I know very definitely I faced this when I lost my husband in Africa. We were new missionaries on the mission field just six weeks and were having our welcoming service when there was an explosion of a portable generator. My husband was severely burned. We placed him in a makeshift hospital room in a small village facility. There we learned he had a rare type of blood, and his life was much in jeopardy. I felt strongly that God would take care of him, for hundreds of people in Africa and in the States were praying for his healing. But he died one week after the accident.

That was of course the greatest crisis of my life and one that was very difficult to understand. We felt we were doing God's work and had gone where He had sent us. It took me some days to really see through that and to recognize in prayer that the Lord had another plan I knew nothing about. I realized I could not prevent what happened; neither could I let anger and bitterness possess my heart. In prayer the Lord enabled me to give this whole drama to Him and agree that He could make something good out of it. I saw it as total disaster, but He saw it with possibilities that only a wise, loving Heavenly Father could have.

God answered my prayer, but it took time. It also took a different direction from what I had hoped for. After staying in West Africa for about two years, my young daughter and I came home to the States. We remained here for nearly six years, then went back to work in the eastern part of Africa. Toward the end of our first term there we were invited to return to the area where we had previously served. We journeyed to West Africa for the dedication of a library that was a memorial to the fallen missionary. I met numbers of Africans who were involved in pastoral ministries and some in official capacities who told me that as youngsters, they had knelt at my husband's grave to commit their lives to the Lord's service. They were grateful to God for the missionary who died in the line of duty. Although it was some years after the accident, I began to see God's answer to my prayer. He had indeed fashioned something significant out of what I considered to be total chaos.

As a widow I continued in missions and other areas of the Lord's service. I prayed many times for a godly companion with whom to share my life. God answered that prayer with a resounding yes. Twenty years after my loss He gave me a wonderful Christian husband who had lost his first wife to terminal illness. Our spouses had been related, so we knew each other well. Twenty years was not too long to wait for God's perfect will!

Let me be quick to say I have not learned everything I need to know about prayer. But I am enjoying my time with God, and I learn something new each day.

RICHARD J. FOSTER

Richard J. Foster teaches widely about spiritual life. He is founder and chair of Renovare, a spiritual-formation organization based in Wichita, Kansas, and Jack and Barbara Lee Distinguished Professor of Spiritual Formation at Azusa Pacific University in Azusa, California. He is the author of Celebration of Discipline: The Path to Spiritual Growth *(1978), which has sold more than one million copies and been translated into eight languages;* The Challenge of the Disciplined Life: Christian Reflections on Money, Sex, and Power *(1983); and* Prayer: Finding the Heart's True Home *(1992). Foster, a Quaker, was professor of Theology and writer in residence at Friends University, in Wichita, from 1979 to 1992. He, his wife, Carolyn, and their two children Joel and Nathan live in Wichita.*

Prayer is interacting with God about what God and I are doing together. This morning, for example, I went out and jogged; often I pray when I jog, and become aware of God. After a half an hour or so of that, I end up in a little prayer chapel I use while I'm staying at the university here. First I open my mind to the Scripture for a while and then I pray for my family, prayers of protection for them. Then I try entering what French author Madame Guyan calls beholding Lord—in other words, being open to God's presence. That means listening and interacting in any way that seems appropriate. The idea of course is to bring prayer into every experience in life. That is the larger sense in which prayer goes with you throughout the day—it's in the meeting that I just had, in the class that I'll have with students tonight. Missionary Frank Lawbouch said, "I want to learn how to live, so that to see someone is to pray for them."

I try to bring the experience of prayer into the ordinary experiences of life. As I move through the day, I'm trying to be aware of God's presence—trying to be centered in his life and ways, seeking to view each situation as "the sacrament of the present moment," to use French author Jean Pierre de Caussade's phrase. De Caussade describes the life of prayer this way: "The soul, light as a feather, fluid as water, innocent as a child, responds to every movement of grace like a floating balloon." It is Brother Lawrence's idea of "the practice of the presence of God." So I try to bring myself to embrace that reality throughout the day, and then I also seek to enter the night with God. Brother Lawrence said, "Those who have the gale of the Holy Spirit go forward, even in sleep."

But we do all of this with a kind of lightness. I know as I've described it, it sounds a little heavy, but it really isn't. There's a lot of laughter and a lot of fun. A lot of enjoyment of life goes on as we're walking with God through the activities of the day.

I pray to God, the Creator of all things, the Sustainer of all things, and the Redeemer of all things. It is a personal I-Thou relationship. I am entering into an interaction between the Infinite Spirit of the Universe and a finite human spirit. And how that works we don't fully understand, but that it does work is something that has been witnessed by centuries of people.

I use both spontaneous prayers and set prayers. Right now I'm actually writing prayers myself as a spiritual exercise. Let me share one with you. I call this one "Prayer in the Night":

I'm wide awake and it's three A.M., Lord.
I'm unable to turn off my mind.
I keep going over and over the events of the day.
I worry about what I said and did
Reconstructing conversations and encounters in a thousand
    different ways.
I wish I could turn off my mind.
I need sleep but it's like the accelerator of my mind
Is racing, racing, racing.
God, why don't you let me sleep?
I guess I'm supposed to feel pious at a time like this and pray
But I don't want to pray, I want to sleep.
Why can't I turn off my mind? I'm so tired.
God, can't you simply induce sleep, the great cosmic
    tranquilizer?
I guess I wouldn't want that, even if it were possible, but
I do want to sleep.
God, why can't I sleep? Why can't I sleep?

Then a little later in the morning these words came
to me:

Shalom, my child, Shalom.
You are anxious for many things.
Rest. Rest. Rest in my love.
Sleep is not necessary if you will
Rest in my love.

Now, did God speak to me? Well, I don't know exactly, but it did seem like a right response to my situation, and it taught me to rest in God. I suppose if people
were really to press me on it, I would say that God truly
does communicate with us, but exactly how I don't
know. I mean, I cannot fully answer the whole question
of how a finite spirit can be in communion with the Infinite Spirit of the Universe. But I, and many others
have experienced it.

Sometimes I use written prayers, such as the Book of Common Prayer, and other books of writings. I have a class right now in which students are using John Baillie's *Diary of Private Prayers* as a way of leading them into their own prayers. I suppose if I were to list one prayer that is a key prayer for me, it would be the Jesus prayer: "Lord, Jesus Christ, Son of God, have mercy on me, a sinner." That is the most basic prayer, and I use it often. Of course there are many other prayers—the Serenity Prayer, the Saint Francis prayer—that are very good prayers, but personally I like the Jesus prayer.

In one sense we are praying always, but I do have a set time of prayer—perhaps thirty minutes to an hour. And there are other times when I might take a little day of prayer in solitude. Often I'll connect that to the seasons: winter, spring, summer, fall. Or I'll do it in connection with some trip I'm taking: I'll stay a couple of days extra and spend the time in private retreat.

I pray both silently and out loud. Certainly there is silent prayer, the prayer of quiet. I think of Kierkegaard's famous sentence: "A man prayed and first he thought that prayer was talking, but he became more and more quiet until in the end he realized that prayer was listening." Certainly prayer often goes beyond words, but many times words are used. Today I did both. Prayer in silence and then spoken out loud. It doesn't really matter, does it? I mean, God isn't hard of hearing.

Meditation is one of the most basic forms of listening prayer. Usually it's tied to a passage of Scripture. Other times it can move more deeply into what is usually thought of as contemplation, in which, as French author J. N. Grou prayed, "Oh Divine Master teach me this mute language that says so much." So, there is silence, listening prayer, and meditation. These must be a regular part of our prayer experience because it isn't just a matter of us talking, it's a matter of listening to God's voice in his wondrous, loving, all-embracing silence.

During the experience of prayer I often gain focus, sinking down into the life of God in such a way that I can become comfortable in that posture. And out of that I seek to live my day. I find I am more on target and have a greater sense of confidence and strength in what I am doing, so that I am living the day out of the guidance that prayer gives me.

When I pray, I ask for guidance, blessings, forgiveness—many things. And I allow the prayer experience to flow out of my living experience. This isn't an inferior way to pray. Jesus, for example, in the Lord's Prayer, taught people to ask, and so we do. But our prayer work is also disciplined by the Spirit so that it isn't selfish—that is, filled with the self.

The way we know it is God who is working with us is this: God draws and encourages; Satan condemns and pushes. Let me give you a little story about that. When I was at another university, I brought a group together to debate a big issue. They arrived and debated the problem, and I thought that we would settle it in one meeting, but we didn't. The problem got worse and worse and worse. I went back to my office afterward and thought to myself, "This is terrible; it is going to take months to solve this problem." So I started a prayer of complaint to God. "God," I prayed, "I don't have time for all of this. It'll take months to solve this problem." Then I entered a time of listening, and it was as if God was saying, "I didn't ask you to solve this problem in the first place. Relax, and this matter will be cared for in time." Now, letting go of it saved me an immense amount of work. And after a few years the issue has been resolved. So we live in that guidance, that sense of rightness in which we've heard the *Kol Yahweh*, the voice of the Lord.

People who really pray—not people who just analyze prayer or dissect it, but who actually *do* it—become more loving, more sensitive to other people. I've watched this happen, and I think I'm reflecting not only my own experience but the experience of many other people. Prayer enlarges our ability to embrace other people. The class I'm teaching right now, for example, is an incredibly cross-cultural group. We have Afro-Americans, we have Anglos, we have Koreans, we have Japanese, we have Latinos. The mix is wonderful and because these people pray, their hearts are enlarged toward one another, even with all the cultural differences. I guess, to put it in a phrase, we become more loving toward others.

Of necessity, love of God eventuates in love of neighbor. The two great commandments are really one. Prayer *always* has a social dimension to it. Prayer, to be real prayer, does not take us out of the world; it sends us *into* the world and excites our endeavors to heal the world. I had a prayer group for three years in Wichita, Kansas, and the task we undertook was to pray for the city. Doing so made many change the kinds of things they did, especially for the poor. Learning how to pray for areas of crime, areas of drugs, areas of prostitution was really interesting. In the third year, I told the group I'd been asking God to give us some special direction. I told them we ought to pray to reduce the crime rate by 10 percent—just by the work of prayer, and the action would come out of that. Well, around Christmas someone did a special three-year study of crime in the city, and it had dropped *33 percent*. On television they asked the chief of police why this was so, and he couldn't figure out why. Who knows why? I can't prove that our little prayer group had anything to do with reducing that crime rate, but it *is* amazing sometimes what will happen when people actually begin to pray.

I also gave my class ideas such as going to the

schoolgrounds of their city and walking around, praying prayers of protection for the children. We know where the areas of real need are, so I would urge the class to go there and be with people and see what happens. All the time they would be praying. For example, they would get on the bus and ride anonymously, praying to the backs of the heads of people. We tried lots of things; they were all fun. Prayer doesn't have to be stuffy, in a church, or formalized. I would encourage people as they go jogging to bless the homes as they go by and the people in them, to ask for the good to rise up and the evil to dissipate.

There is a lot of work that I do that's unrelated to prayer: committee meetings, writing, lectures. I strive to bring prayer into all of those experiences. For example, when I wrote *Money, Sex, and Power*, I decided that I wanted to see how the actual writing experience itself could be sacramental. So I would take communion each morning, and then would try to see how my hands on the keyboard and the flow of ideas could be a sacramental act, God's life coming to me through that process. I think I moved through that experience with greater power, and a greater sense of the presence of God, than any I had done before that time.

One time I was in a committee meeting. I decided I wanted to learn a little more about prayer in that meeting. Now we were just talking business, but there was one lady in the group whose shoulders were kind of slumped. I decided she would be a "special intention" for prayer. So I prayed for her silently throughout the meeting. While we were carrying on business, I noticed that she kept speaking in these barbs at one young couple in the group, and I thought to myself, "I'm not doing very good." Well, the meeting lasted about two hours, and when we finished and were ready to break up, this woman turned to the group and, breaking into tears, said, "Would somebody pray for me before we leave?" And then out came the need. And what was especially tender was that this young couple she had criticized came over to her and placed their hands on her and prayed for her. I felt like taking off my shoes, for it was holy ground.

Over the years prayer has moved from me being the actor, the talker, to more and more me being the receiver, the listener. There is still plenty of talk, and I'm still an active participant, but I've become more and more interested in receiving and in being available to kind of waste time for God. I don't have to produce, I don't even have to say anything; I can just rest in God's presence.

Recently I was with a group of writers on the Pacific Coast of Canada. We took our mid-morning break, and there were some canoes on the shore, so I got in one to go over to a tiny promontory—it was too small to call an island. I paddled out there and docked this little canoe. It was full of trees, so I explored it for a while. I was just having a good time; I wasn't trying to be religious. Up on top of this little island somebody had built a platform, and there was an old chair on it. So I sat in the chair and I was just being quiet, just enjoying the beauty of the trees and the sky and the water and so forth. Then I remembered what Carolyn, my wife, had said to me as I left on this particular trip. She said, "I want you to come home refreshed." So I prayed and said, "God, refresh me." And there was this response, "I want to teach you Sabbath prayer." I leaned forward and said, "Oh, I don't know exactly what that means. You'll have to teach me." And there came these words: "Be still. Rest. Shalom." Those three phrases. So I tried to enter into that for a period of time. And then I began to worry about getting back to start the meeting. And again there

were the same words: "Be still. Rest. Shalom." So I set-
tled back in listening prayer, resting prayer, what one
writer calls the prayer of quiet.

After fifteen minutes or so I had this hyperresponsibil-
ity that I've got to get back; people are going to wonder
where I am, they're going to be worried that maybe I
tipped over in the canoe. And again those words came
over me: "Be still. Rest. Shalom." Then, as a writer, I got
to thinking, "This experience is so wonderful, I've got to
write it down, I've got to capture it; I can't remember it
all." And then again those words: "Be still. Rest. Shalom." So I entered back into Sabbath prayer. So finally,
when I felt that the experience had finished, I went
back, and it was funny because the group had gone right
on with the meeting without me. They didn't even notice I was gone! It was a lovely experience of learning
the prayer of rest, in which I don't have to be so worried
about accomplishment.

GEORGE GALLUP, JR.

George Gallup, Jr. is chairman of the George H. Gallup International Institute, co-chairman of the Gallup Organization, Inc., and executive director of the Princeton Religion Research Center. He serves on the boards of Religion in American Life, Living Church Associates, the Trinity Episcopal School for Ministry, and Oklahoma Christian University. His books include America's Search for Faith, *with David Poling (1980);* Adventures in Immortality, *with William Proctor (1982);* The American Catholic People, *with Jim Castelli (1987);* The People's Religion, *with Jim Castelli (1989);* Varieties of Prayer, *with Margaret Poloma (1991); and* The Saints Among Us, *with Timothy Jones (1992). He and his wife, Kingsley, have three children and live in Princeton, N.J.*

I like what Teresa of Avila said about prayer. "The life of prayer is just the love of God and a liking to be with Him." It means that prayer is a pervasive thing; it's sort of a substratum to life—a partnership with God, if you will. It suggests to me an ongoing sense of the presence of God, which is the ultimate goal in developing prayer. It involves talking to God both silently and aloud, and more importantly, *listening* to God. Prayer is not just a matter of seeking God but of bearing in mind that God is always seeking us. It also suggests the need to put God first in prayer.

I pray to God the Father through His Son, Jesus Christ. As I grow in my faith journey, I have become more focused in this respect. In the past I prayed to a more nebulous spirit; it was not as distinct as it is now. I call upon Jesus Christ and the Holy Spirit as well, because I believe that they are part of the Godhead.

Prayer has been important to me as long as I can remember, but I have become increasingly more focused in terms of whom I pray to, the frequency and types of prayer, and the fact that I don't just pray in a crisis but rather thank God during those times when life seems to be very good. I've also discovered that the more I pray, the more I want to pray. It is natural in some ways to believe in the supernatural dimension, and when you get yourself in that zone or dimension, it is much easier to accept the inner life and that God is speaking to you. It becomes much more natural.

I pray in short bursts but also in longer periods, when I sit quietly and listen. I pray in the morning, at various points during the day, and in bed when I'm reviewing the day and getting set for the next. I pray before business and board meetings. I pray in small groups and at church. I pray with Kinney (my spouse); usually we read something from a book such as Oswald Chambers's *My Utmost for His Highest*. I always say grace at meals now, and I do this in public because I think it's a good witness. People are sort of stunned and stare at you in disbelief, but I think it's a good thing to do.

The Lord's Prayer is my favorite prayer because it covers all bases. Another favorite is the Jesus Prayer, because the one word *Jesus* says it all for me. It helps one to center and not get distracted; it helps one to listen. Saint Francis's prayer is another favorite. Another that I like is, "Lord, make us masters of ourselves so that we can be servants of others. Take our minds and think through them, take our lips and speak through them, take our hearts and set them afire." It reminds us that we have to get it straight with the Lord before we can effectively reach out to other people. I've tried to trace that prayer, but it's anonymous. I also collect prayers in a notebook; I'm sort of a prayer collector. I make up prayers as well.

I use different prayers at different times, and in them I usually incorporate one or more of the different aspects of prayer—adoration, thanksgiving, petition, confession, and intercession. I used to concentrate more on thanksgiving and petition, but now I'm trying to do more in the area of adoration and intercession, and in that regard I think it's important to pray first for those persons who have hurt you most and are the hardest to pray for; I believe a vital part of prayer teaches us to forgive.

Through prayer I've seen a vision of what I believe God wants in my life. I believe that God gives us a word for the day, and that if we accept this as being of God, incredible things can happen. I try to keep God's word for me as a constant reference point during the day, and as I try to build a sense of partnership with God in confronting the many problems of life, I increasingly feel the presence of God. The more I accept, the more I believe, and the more I feel that God is guiding me. And afterward I feel empowered. Sometimes I feel as if I'm on a high. Prayer gives me a sense of peace now, and the assurance of future peace, even after death. I feel confirmed and empowered. I believe God talks to me, although not out loud. I believe that God listens, although His way of answering me may not be what I expect or desire.

Prayer helps me to find deeper meaning in painful crises. It affects my relationships considerably, giving me patience, helping me to put important things first, helping me to see that other people are children of God and to be more sensitive to where they are coming from. Prayer affects my work a lot. I pray that I will do the kind of work that will help to build the Kingdom of God and that the research of the Gallup Organization can be used to help people and to move society ahead in ways that are pleasing to God.

Prayer in itself is a form of action that can help society and other people. I believe the power of prayer is the most important source of power in the world, yet most people do not tap into this power. One cannot know God unless one walks with Him. Prayer is very important for a life of faith and brings us into touch with all of humanity, with people one doesn't know. And the more I seek to be obedient through prayer, the more I trust God is working in me and through me.

I'm involved in groups that are called Covenant groups; I've been involved in these groups for probably ten years. These were developed by Roberta Hestafuss, the president of Easton College in Saint Davids, Pennsylvania. They usually last about an hour and a half and are broken into three periods. The first is a period of sharing; we talk about anything to bring people out. We find out if something has happened in your life and so forth. The second period is one of praying the Bible. It's not really for studying the Bible—it's not about saying, "What's the source of this or that?"—but it's about using the Bible passages to see how they relate to people's present problems. The third and final half hour is devoted to prayer for each other and with each other; it's both silent prayer and aloud prayer. We meet once a week, but there are breaks; it's not just relentlessly around the year. It's important to have breaks. We break usually after eight weeks because otherwise it becomes a chore.

The central purpose of these Covenant groups is to teach people to pray, to feel comfortable with praying out loud, and to give prayer the time it deserves. That's a great need in our society. I think the clergy makes assumptions about where people are in their prayer lives; they think people are much farther along than they are. These groups have really made a difference in my own faith journey.

There's something particularly powerful about prayer in a group; there is a sort of corrective mechanism. When you're discussing things and you're praying for things; it's important to have other people's insights, and their prayer, and their contact with God. You can bounce things off people; they can say, "Well, George, really; perhaps *this* is what is happening." In a sense they're a sounding board. You could go off on the wrong tack if you're alone, but when you're with a group, it keeps you from falling into error in your perceptions of what kinds of things you should be doing.

I think Covenant groups are a healthy kind of setting for prayer. Small groups are important to those who find the church setting too impersonal and can't really open up. Our group comprises ten persons of all different ages and backgrounds. Since this particular group is related to my church, we're all Episcopalians, but I've been in other groups with Catholics. Small groups as a whole—going beyond the ones that have just a religious dimension—are exceedingly important. We live in a disjointed, impersonal society, a fragmented society, and small groups provide one way for people to come back together.

ANN GARVIN

Ann Garvin is president of Church Women United and a member of the African Methodist Episcopal Church. A retired school teacher, she runs a consulting company and is active in a wide range of community activities. She is a former president of Women in Community Service. She and her husband live in Topeka, Kansas.

I define prayer as talking to God. I address Him in different ways—sometimes as God our Creator, sometimes as Holy God, sometimes as Sustainer, sometimes as Father or Lord. While I almost always end my prayers in the name of Jesus, I pray to God. I pray all during the day, when I wake up at night, and whenever I feel the need to say something to God. Sometimes it might be a plea or a request and sometimes it might be a thank-you. Sometimes I pray just to say that now I understand why something has happened. Sometimes I pray after I read something, when somebody sends me something, or when someone tells me something. There's no regularity about it. Prayer comes in many different forms. But when it happens, you know it.

Prayer first became important to me when I was finishing up my formal education and as an early wife and mother. By that time all the things that I'd learned in Sunday school, my youth organizations, and so forth began to have more of a personal meaning. I guess that's because that was the stage of my life where I needed to be more responsible but didn't have much guidance. I became more conscious of what I was saying when I prayed, and I began to pray more often. I began to grow in my meditations and my daily Bible readings and the supplementary kinds of things you do that lead to prayer.

In the readings from time to time I find things that strike me as pertaining to whatever my prayer concern is at that particular time. Sometimes it might be what I'm praying about most recently, or sometimes it might be something that I prayed about some time ago but don't feel like I've gotten the answer to yet. A lot of times I have to pray about something more than once; it becomes a regular part of my prayers until I feel that it has been resolved. Or when I have to make a presentation, I often sit down and go back through the readings I've done. I look for things that I think I may have missed; they may not have been as meaningful to me because I wasn't ready, or because circumstances were different than they were at the time I originally did the reading.

Over the years I've become more interested in reading other people's opinions on prayer and books on prayer. And it can help even when we listen to other people pray. I have heard people pray in public, and I can tell from their prayer that they have a lot of concerns, that they have a lot of depth to their personality that I was not aware of, because I had no reason to be aware of it otherwise. Listening to people pray tells you a lot about that person and about his or her personality. But it goes both ways. Just as it shows depth, it shows lack of depth. I've heard people pray who have written their prayers out, and with some of them it sounds as though the prayer were spontaneous; it's obvious that it was *their* prayer, and I'm amazed and delighted at the kinds of things that they're concerned about. Then there are other people, and it seems like there's nothing personal in their prayer; it's almost like they wrote a speech. You *have* to make your prayer personal.

What do I personally pray for? I pray for guidance. I pray for God to use me to do whatever it is that God wants me to do. I pray that God will let me do it the way that God wants me to do it. I pray that when I'm trying to help somebody, God will show me how to do it, give me words to say or whatever actions I'm to do that are going to be helpful. If it's a situation that I've been concerned about and have not been able to figure out one angle or one piece of, I find there just comes a time when all of a sudden I know exactly what I'm supposed to do or what was missing.

So I've become more aware of when my prayers are answered, whereas before I often wouldn't realize it until sometime after the answer had actually come. However, sometimes it's really, really obvious—if you are asking for something concrete, you can't help but know it when the answer comes. For example, sometimes I find myself too busy and in a rush, rush, rush; my stress level is up, and I can't find something. I will look and look and look until I think I've looked in all the possible places; finally I just become utterly stressed and realize that I'm trying to do this all by myself. Then I will say aloud, "All right, Lord, please help me," or "It's up to you." Then I'll forget about it, and sometimes within five minutes I'll walk right to it. And that's after I will have been looking for over an hour!

Sometimes I wake up in the middle of the morning and I'm not particularly stressed—I just am wide awake—and I will lie there for a little while and start praying. After I've said whatever I want to, I will find I'm calm and able to go right to sleep. If I don't go right to sleep, I'm at least aware that I am more relaxed. A lot of the time I pray because I *know* that that kind of calmness will come.

Some people pray for the president and the governor and so on. I do that occasionally, especially if it's an obviously tense situation. And a lot of times I do pray about my relationship with other people. It varies; it might be a personal relationship, it might be a group relationship where I'm part of a group, it might involve my particular role with a group as a leader or as just a member. But most of the time I pray for things like "Let us be more sensitive and kind and good to one another." I do that more so than I do about individual leaders, even more so than I do about issues.

When I do pray about issues, which is frequently the case, I pray that we will find a way to resolve our problems with upbringing of the children, with social justice, and with social-rehabilitation situations, and that we'll get over this business of some facet of the society always having to abuse another facet and keep it down in order to feel more powerful. My prayer is that God will in some way improve the self-esteem of the group that's doing the abusing so that they'll no longer find it necessary to do that. I just pray that God will give the people being abused the strength and know-how to get out of such situations. I'm praying for God to tell them how to change and to give them the ability to recognize what they need to do and the strength to do it.

RAJSHRI GOPAL

Rajshri Gopal is a Sunday school teacher, tour guide, and member of the Sri Venkateswara Temple in Pittsburgh, the oldest Hindu temple in the United States. She and her husband have lived in Pittsburgh for more than thirty years and were founding members of the temple. They have three daughters and a grandson.

Prayer is a communication with God. Sometimes it is no words at all; it's just thoughts. Sometimes it involves words, and then I might use prayers that I already know—some of the Sanskrit prayers which are so well thought out, so meaningful.

Every morning after the shower I walk into the place in the house where there's a shrine. In the previous house it was just a little closet; in the present house we have a little room. It's very, very nice, and quiet. I go in there. I always burn an oil lamp; it's traditional. There are pictures of Hindu gods and some statues that are very artistic metal icons. The pictures of the deities are about two feet by eighteen inches. I have both gods, Shiva and Vishnu. A lot of households, if they're very traditional, have one sect, either Shiva or Vishnu.

In Hinduism there is the trinity. The Creator God is one of them. Brahma is the creator. After creation He remains the foundation for all living things. He is looked on as the father of the universe. As the protector, the preserver, he is Vishnu, the second part of the trinity. And then again, He is the dissolver, known as Shiva.

In Hinduism, God alone is eternal, so all creation will have an end. That means that there are many creations, one after the other. Each of these creations lasts for many, many millions of years. But when the time comes and that creation has to end, the stage is set for a re-creation, so God dissolves the present. If you think of a person's death, for instance, what happens is the body deteriorates, but the soul lives on. In the Hindu religion the soul is everlasting. So the material things deteriorate and change form, but the soul lives on. On a very large scale the entire universe is dissolved, but the spiritual things live on. Only the material things are separated from the spiritual. That is what is called the last dissolution, *Samhara*. The stage is set for re-creation, and this goes on for many cycles. These cycles are known as *yugas*.

So God plays different roles. Subconsciously you remember that God is one. But if you want to make it easier, to make things come closer to this big, abstract thing, to attributes of God, such as eternal, omniscient, omnipotent, omnipresent, you are allowed (and actually encouraged) to have personal gods, to pray to any one of the roles at any time. So I might call the name of Shiva in the morning and then Vishnu in the afternoon.

I light incense—not every day, but occasionally. Daily I light the lamp. I sit there and I meditate. I pray for different lengths of time on different days. Sometimes I'm praying and a phone call comes, so I get up and I might not go back. Other times it's very quiet and I don't have anything to do right away. I never look at the clock, but I'd say I spend twenty, twenty-five minutes in meditation—as much as possible. Then when I come out of meditation, I'm very calm. I sit for a few minutes and then I do the ritualistic, not kneeling exactly, but bowing down with your forehead touching the ground. I finish off like that.

I'm fifty-four years old, so this is the time, according to the Hindus, for religion. The first twenty-five years you devote to student life. The next twenty-five you are a householder; that is when you contribute the most to society, give for all the good causes, take a spouse and have a household, and responsibly raise children. And then when you settle the children down and see them married, it's "forest-dweller stage," the time for philosophy and religion and those things. Literally, back in those days they went off to the forest. The wife went along with the husband and later, when he renounces the world and becomes the *sanyasi*, the wife returns to the son's house.

I have these crystal beads I bought in India in one of the temples. There are 108 beads. One hundred and eight is a very holy number. I use this to repeat some attributes of God. Some of the chantings, the prayers, are very nice because you say the name of God; for instance if I'm praying to Ganesha, who is one of the deities, I would use various names of Ganesha. It helps your mind remember the attributes. For instance, to Vishnu we pray, "Thou art the father of the universe, Thou art the form of light, You are an ocean of mercy," and so forth. When you are chanting these things, you remember what the deity is. Sometimes I think (this is from the Scriptures), "All the souls are like different pearls or beads and you are the thread that runs through all of them. You are the cause of the universe. You are the cause that maintains the universe."

I get answers to prayer when my suffering goes away, when there's a solution. This happens even with the smaller things I pray for. For instance if I lose something, I pray, "Ganesha, every time I have troubled you, you found it for me. Please do it again." And then I might find my precious thing that I left somewhere, anywhere at all. With prayer sometimes I feel that everything is going to be all right; I've surrendered my problems. Even when I go to the temple, no matter how hard things are, I feel, "Oh, God is watching, so everything is going to be all right." It's very strange that I might be so worried, but then when I go there, I feel okay.

Ganesha is the personification of the Sanskrit letter OM that looks like the number three with a little tail in the middle. This is a very sacred sound. A lot of times in Scriptures they say, "There was the sound in the beginning." *That* is what the OM is. Every day before you say the name of God, you say OM. For instance, if I say, "OM, Shiva," that means that I'm invoking Shiva. OM starts every prayer, every sacred name. In meditation yogis use it. Red, blue, and yellow are the primary colors. If you have these three, you can mix them in different proportions and you can get any color you want. OM has the three important sounds all inside of it. It is *ahh* and *oo* and *mm*. *Ah* and *oo* become *o* in OM. When you say OM in meditation, you're supposed to get your mind filled; you get control of your mental and physical and intellectual self. That's why you say OM in the beginning of meditation.

There's a very beautiful concept about Ganesha. Ganesha is also worshiped as the son of Shiva and is the primary deity even before we worship other deities. At a music concert the first song will be offered to Ganesha. In a dance concert the first item will be about Ganesha. In a wedding Ganesha's name always comes first. He is known as the troubleshooter. Once you have used His name, the whole event will go well. He is the remover of hindrances, obstacles.

Mostly Hindu prayer is individualistic, but for functions like a new year or some holiday we all assemble at the temple in the big hall, on the carpet in the lotus posture. There are no shoes. In the center of the hall will be the portable icons that come out of the shrine. The hall will be decorated with flowers and jewelry and silk, and incense will be burned and lights will be shone. Then people might sing together or a few people might sing one after the other. Then there will be a prayer offered, and when everyone stands up, it's all finished. This is an example of a group prayer, but most of the time when we go to the temple, it's only the family or maybe a few friends who come along with you—a handful. It's all done individually. The priest offers the light and does the chanting, and then you close your eyes and you have your quiet moments. Before you return, they give you some *prasad*—it literally means "tranquillity that you receive by coming here." Usually the *prasad* is a little bit of raisins mixed with cashews, or it might be a fruit. Whatever its form, they always give you something.

If somebody has really done something bad to me, during ordinary times I will say, "I don't understand what's going on." But during prayers, when I pray for everybody—for my mother, for my mother-in-law, for my children—I might even think of this person and say, "Bless her." But not too often, even though I know it does help your forgiveness and you grow spiritually to a higher plane.

The Hindu outlook is very broad. We teach the little children at the temple one prayer that says that all living beings should be happy. That means that we are praying for the entire universe, all the people of the universe. It's a way of emphasizing the universal brotherhood. Hinduism is a very liberal kind of religion; they accept all religions as true, as different paths to the same goal, as different chapters of the same book. This sublime view comes forth from the *Upanishads*.

The Vedas are the four books that Hindus receive all

their beliefs from. The *Upanishads* are the end part and the most philosophical and secular part of the Vedas. There are hymns, and there are rituals. But the last part is very, very philosophical, very secular in nature. When I talk about secular, I mean emphasizing the oneness of God and no names: "The one without a second, the one who is true, who is conscious, who is blissful in nature." They never mention Vishnu or Shiva or anything like that. They say, "The One."

BILLY GRAHAM

Billy Graham, a Southern Baptist minister, is chairman of the board and CEO of the Billy Graham Evangelistic Association. He has preached to more people in live audiences than anyone else in history: 180 million people in 180 countries. He has been on the Gallup Poll's list of Most Admired Men every year since he first appeared on it more than forty years ago. Graham has written seventeen books, including Storm Warning *(1992) and* How to Be Born Again *(1977). He and his wife, Ruth, have five children, nineteen grandchildren, and four great-grandchildren.*

Paul told us to "pray without ceasing" (1 Thess. 5:17). I think that, in a sense, all who really know Christ *do* pray without ceasing. I pray all the time; it is something that's going on all the time within me. I pray while I'm walking, talking, lying down, whatever.

No evangelist can ever have God's blessing on his ministry until he realizes his total dependence on the Holy Spirit. That means we need to prepare by prayer. I have often been asked the secret of evangelistic crusades, and I have said there are three secrets: (1) prayer; (2) prayer; (3) prayer.

A great deal of prayer is necessary in my work, and a great deal of humility, for you realize that you depend entirely on the spirit of God. That's the reason we put all of the emphasis on prayer in our crusades. We ask thousands of people in every area where we go to join in prayer groups and Bible-study groups and pray not only for me but for themselves and their city.

I find myself praying while I'm talking to people. I say, "Lord, help me to say the right thing," and "Lord, help me not to be offensive; help me to say the thing that will encourage people to believe." I believe that when one is saying something consciously, your subconscious can still be praying. Even while I'm preaching, I'm praying. And I'm saying, "Lord help me to say the right thing. Let it sink into their hearts. May it accomplish your purpose." I believe that while I am preaching the Gospel, another voice is speaking: the voice of the Holy Spirit.

I use prayer and meditation to recharge my spiritual batteries. There have been times in my life when I was overwhelmed with conviction of sin and have gone out alone and confessed everything I could ever think of and asked God to search my heart deeply, and I found things there that I didn't know were there.

My wife and I live in a very remote part of America in the mountains of North Carolina. There's a little place where I walk or run or jog, and it's about a tenth of a mile each way. We have two dogs who accompany me. One of them will go with me all the way, but the other has gotten so used to the routine that now he sits down in the middle and just watches me go both ways. That run is where I do a lot of praying and confessing. But I also have stated periods of prayer. My wife and I, for example, read the Bible every night before we go to bed and then we pray together. Then I usually get up around seven and am usually finished with breakfast by eight. I watch the news and then I have my devotional period. I read the Bible, and sometimes read a little commentary on it. As I read, I think of things to pray for—besides those things and individuals I already have on my prayer list.

The Bible talks about praying in season and out of season (2 Tim. 4:2). We need prayer both in our work and in our everyday lives. I heard about a young president of an East Coast company. He instructed his secretary not to disturb him because he had an important appointment. The chairman of the board came in and said, "I want to see Mr. Jones." The secretary answered, "I'm terribly sorry, he cannot be disturbed; he has an important appointment." And the chairman became very angry. He banged open the door and saw the president of his corporation on his knees in prayer. The chairman softly closed the door and asked the secretary, "Is this usual?" And she said, "Yes, he does that every morning." And the chairman of the board said, "No wonder I come to him for advice."

I feel that we need voluntary prayer in the schools of the United States. We have had the issue of praying in school since the Supreme Court ruling back in the early sixties. I am against prayers that have been devised by the government for students to pray, but I *am* for voluntary prayer. To me, forbidding prayer in schools is a little bit hypocritical in that the Congress has a chapel, the Senate has a chapel, and the president takes his oath of office with his hand on the Bible. Today the Bible is taught in the schools in Poland and in certain parts of the former Soviet Union. So I have suggested that we hang the Ten Commandments in every school room to serve as a solid reminder that there are moral guidelines. I said this publicly in front of Chief Justice Warren Burger, and we talked about it afterward. Even if this cannot happen, at least students can still pray in their hearts; no court ruling can alter that.

We are living in dangerous times, and if there were ever a time that we need to pray, it's now. More can be done by prayer than anything else. Prayer is our greatest weapon because when we pray, we are turning in humble trust and faith to the living God, Who loves us and gave His Son to die for our sins.

When I pray before any group, it is my prayer that every single person in the place will leave praying a prayer of repentance and belief. I also pray for a new beginning for America. I believe we could be in the beginning of that new beginning right now and that our best days could be before us, if we repent and turn to Christ.

ANDREW M. GREELEY

Andrew M. Greeley is a priest of the archdiocese of Chicago and a professor of sociology at the University of Chicago. He is also a best-selling novelist, with more than twenty million copies of his books in print. His books include The Catholic Myth: The Behavior and Beliefs of American Catholics *and* Fall from Grace. *In 1984 Greeley established a one-million-dollar endowed chair in Roman Catholic Studies at the University of Chicago. In 1986 he established a one-million-dollar Inner-City Catholic School Fund providing scholarships and financial support to schools in the archdiocese of Chicago with a minority enrollment of more than 50 percent.*

Prayer has always been important to me. It took me a long time to figure out how to do it and to realize that what works for you is the way you should be praying. No formula for spirituality, however good in theory, is necessarily what you should be doing. It took a rather long time for prayer to become deeply important to me, but still it's not as important as it should be.

I'm not part of a prayer group or anything of that sort. I'm not at all opposed to that; it's just something that hasn't happened. Nor do I use set prayers; they simply don't respond to my needs at this stage of life. And while I've written about the sociology of mysticism, I'm not a mystic. I know people who are and I've read the literature, but that's not me. And it's not necessary to be one. John Shea, who is a mystic, says there are all different kinds of contacts with God, and there's no point in thinking that one is better than the other.

I have three kinds of prayer that make a difference to me. One is a journal of reflections that I write in my computer. The second is liturgy. The third is writing poetry.

The God to whom I write all my reflections is Lady Wisdom or Mary the Mother of Jesus. Sometimes she's one, sometimes she's the other. I sometimes address her as "My Love." My research has convinced me that thinking of God as a womanly God is much more useful for the spiritual life of men than it is for women. I myself find that to be so. Of course God is both male and female and neither male nor female.

The image of God has no effect on the spiritual life of women, but it does have an impact on the spiritual life of men. For me it's a cross-gender thing. It's hard for a man, I think, to permit himself to feel intimate with a manly God. Not impossible, but it's much easier to feel a sense of intimacy with a womanly God. Sometimes in my journal I'm impressed and depressed with the amount of complaining and griping I do, but then I think that's what a womanly lover is for. They want to hear these complaints from us, they want to hear about what's wrong. That's pushing the metaphor pretty far, but I think it's appropriate.

Some mornings I get up at four. I do my swim and I do my reflections. This makes a big difference in my day. Prayer is a source of reflection and refreshment and orients the day for me. It doesn't always affect what *happens* during the day, but it always gives an orientation to start off with.

I try to do my reflections in the morning because that's when they're most likely to affect the rest of the day. At my house I have rigged up a holy-water font, which I use to remind me to pray. That doesn't remind me for very long, however, and I have learned through the years that someone who is designed the way I am needs things like a holy-water font *and* computer screen to remind them to pray!

As a penalty for my sins I read "Tintern Abbey" and the other stuff of the Victorian era. These guys are all going out to nature in awesome ruins and finding God there. Well, that's fine, and I can find God in a sunset on Lake Michigan. But I'm more interested in the God who lurks in the city and in people. That's a far more difficult and distracting place to encounter Her, but that's our challenge, and it won't do to go off to Tintern Abbey or the Lake District of England or even Grand Beach. Solitude is useful—the more the better—but I can't, and I think many of us can't, build our lives around solitude. We have to find the Lord or Lady Wisdom or whoever in the press of everyday events as well as in solitude. I'm not one of those who's opposed to solitude, but I don't think we can structure our spiritual lives around it.

Often times I don't pray in the middle of commotion. When I do, it is because there is some grace or abundance that makes me reflect on what I'm doing. John Shea said something interesting to me recently: "God works through nature, and it's the purpose of the Church to reveal that to us." That's a wonderful insight into how sacramentality works, that the purpose of the church is to call us to grace in nature.

I now really get a tremendous charge out of liturgy. I have come to be convinced that what we said in the seminary—that the Mass is the center of Catholic life—was true then and certainly is true now in a much deeper sense than we realize. Archbishop Rembert Weakland, of Milwaukee, was quoted somewhere as saying that American Catholics now have a Mass-centered religion as opposed to a pope-centered religion. I don't know how much it was *ever* pope-centered. But it is now more Mass-centered, more Eucharist-centered, than ever before. Even when the Eucharist is done badly, it really sustains Catholics, and when they're away from it, they're really happy to get back to it.

I look forward to the liturgy; I enjoy it. If I go into it confused or depressed, I feel much better when I come out of it. The French sociologist Emile Durkheim was right: it *is* an experience of effervescence. I have learned through the years how to make it a really joyful, pleasant experience for the congregation, especially for the kids. If you do it for the kids, you do it for everybody, and that's contagious for me. In Durkheim's words it effervesces for me. If it's a joyous experience, a comic experience for the people, then it becomes that for me too.

At the center of it, instead of preaching sermons anymore I tell stories. That's enormously effective. People enjoy the stories, they remember them, and if I ever try not to do one, they complain. I came about the importance of stories through the back door. I was first of all a sociologist who discovered the importance of storytelling in passing on religion, and then a novelist who wrote stories about religion, and only at the very end someone who worked up enough nerve to try to do this on Sunday morning.

And then I make special efforts to involve the kids in the Mass; I bring them up along the altar. At the handshake of peace I high-five with them. When we're doing the sprinkling of the water, I make sure that I get water on every kid in the church. It becomes what it ought to be: an extremely pleasant, happy, family event. If you can get people to leave Mass with a smiling face, then you've gotten what it's all about.

Writing poetry is a form of prayer, a form of clarification. Two years ago I lost both my friend Dan Herr and my classmate John Crump, who was the Catholic chaplain at Northwestern, and a number of other friends too, and I really needed to cope with those particular deaths. It took a while, but finally the words began to come and I wrote poems about them. I don't know how good the poems are, but that's not the point; the point is that they are a crystallization, a metaphorization of feelings and conflicts I have. It's a way of externalizing those feelings.

Poetry, art, literature, and music all trigger prayer in me. That's because I'm a Catholic; they *should* do that. If they don't, then there's something missing in our personal development. For our religion is sacramental; that is, it believes that God works everywhere in nature. We believe that grace is everywhere and that nature reveals itself in grace. It's a sanctification of nature. It's a radical difference between us and the other three great religions—Judaism, Islam, and Protestantism—all of whom are afraid of idolatry and tend to emphasize the absent God (Judaism less than the other two). Catholicism early on made its peace with paganism and tends to stress the present God, the God that is everywhere.

When I pray, I look for illumination. Surely the things that occur to me as I sit down to write wouldn't have occurred to me *before*; these reflections are from God and are part of the dialogue with God. Now, that doesn't mean that I imagine God whispering in my ear or that I can hear anything in the ordinary sense of hearing. It's just something I know to be true that I didn't know to be true before. Maybe it's the muse, maybe it's an angel, maybe the muses are angels. But it certainly comes in some fashion from the ultimate other, although not in a mystical way. Saint Paul says that the Spirit speaks to our spirit, and I think what he means—at least translated into modern psychology—is that the Holy Spirit talks to what is most creative, most unique in each of us: the creative imagination.

Over the years prayer has, for me, become more and more personal. I suppose more than anything else it forces me to be open to reconciliation and forgiveness, because you can't engage in dialogue with the intimate other and hold grudges. I always realized that was true, but I guess the kinds of prayer I do now drive it home to me in an even greater way.

HIGH STAR

A Lakota Sioux "singer," or medicine man, who lives in Taos, New Mexico, High Star is a spiritual adviser to both those who belong to Native American traditions and those who do not. He is heavily involved in interfaith work and frequently works with the National Council of Churches. High Star also councils clients referred to him by the American Psychiatric Association.

I'm often asked to describe my tradition. My tradition is a personal journey in spiritual development. But I use Lakota philosophy, which is my background. I mix in a lot of what I understand to be the Tao, because Lakota philosophy and Taoism are so close and so similar. I probably use Taoism as a language more than as a practice. In practice I probably use Lakota traditions as a devotion to the natural order, the universal order. So I blend those two philosophies. In terms of my personal tradition I would say the tradition is one of spiritual development, the constant practice to keep one's alignment with the universal order and with oneself.

Prayer to me really is talking with God. There are many approaches to prayer, but I look at prayer in two ways. One is supplication, which puts a God outside of you and almost anthropomorphizes a being sitting on a throne outside of you. Supplication is always asking for help or resolution from this source greater than you. That seems to me to be a very hierarchical approach, one very much generated by the European or Western mind in terms of a monarchy.

The other form of prayer for me is affirmation or reaffirmation, where you acknowledge fully that you are a manifestation of the greatest power of the universe, the Creator. The affirmation simply says that because you are a manifestation of that reality, whatever qualities you are striving for you already have. But the only way that you can make them real is to affirm them and then live that way.

I would say that living *is* a prayer. To live each day is a prayer in the sense that it's an expression of God. It's the total being that you are, and whether it's spiritual, intellectual, physical, or emotional, it's still the process of living. If you choose dark thoughts, bad thoughts, you're still praying, but you're praying for the dark element as opposed to the light element. The whole process of thinking is actually a prayer because what you hold in your thoughts is what you bring into the world.

I don't look at God as a notion so much as a truth. Asking about the ways in which I pray is a real Western question. Western people always ask about hows and ways and techniques, as though those were the forms of power. Really, the way I pray is to get up every morning and say, "Hi, God, give me a good day."

Of course then we get into rituals, and ritual is the process by which you get people to focus their mind on one objective. There are many prayers using words or actions or dance or art or meditation or contemplation. The easiest way I can say it is that prayer is simply talking to God. You always use the word first. But often you do so in silence. In our Lakota tradition when you have a dance, that's a form of prayer because with your movement to the music or to the songs you're expressing that creative possibility. The ways and means are as varied as your thoughts. You acknowledge that you are part of the Creator. It's greater than you, but it's always a part of you, so in many ways it's like talking to yourself.

Ritual to me is a process whereby everybody agrees to do the same thing. In Lakota tradition we have seven rituals. We have defined terms for them, but they're never done the same way. Each occasion is a whole, spontaneous expression within the confines of what that ritual would be. In Lakota we have the soul-keeping; relationship making; the purification lodge; the girls' puberty ritual, which is called "singing her song"; and then there is "throwing out the ball," which acknowledges her womanhood in the world; Vision Quest; and the Sun Dance. But there's a lot of variation within them, so they're not a liturgy. In liturgy you try to do it the same way every time. In natural philosophies, in natural systems, the ritual only provides a *framework* from which the spontaneous can be achieved. The spontaneous is the way God introduces the new into the world.

When you do rituals like liturgy, you're after basic cause-and-effect relationships. When you combine the two, within the rituals there are a certain amount of activities that are similar from time to time, but what you're after is the *spontaneous* connection to the Spirit, which really can't be predicted or called on by the human mind. If you lay aside the obstructions, then the spontaneous occurrence happens, because the Spirit pervades all things.

In our tradition four of the rituals are feminine in nature, and three of them are masculine in nature. All of these are done by vow. The feminine rituals are all built around childbirth. The masculine rituals are essentially the sweat lodge or the purification lodge, the Vision Quest, and the Sun Dance. Men do not do the feminine rituals, but women sometimes do the masculine rituals. I'll describe the framework of some of these rituals for you.

The basic element of the Sun Dance is a rebirth ceremony where, in the warrior tradition, the man would vow to give back to the Creator, in an offering or sacrifice, the only thing that he owns, and that's the flesh. Much as in the Christian context, where Jesus gave up his life so that others might live; the Sun Dance really is the same thing. The person vows to give flesh back to the Creator by piercing his skin in the chest or arms or back, and he is tied to a tree, which symbolizes the tree of life. The whole act is a rebirth—being born again, you might say, by offering to the Creator what you own, your physical body. So you go through a death process and are reborn again.

You do the Sun Dance as a vow, maybe to help a family member or to achieve a certain amount of healing. Or a person might just want to get it back together again after a crazy life. After you do it once, that should be enough, for the reality is that you're born again. But people get passionate about religion, and many people do it every year. I've done it twice in the last eight years. I did it the second time because after I did it the first time, I took a wrong direction, so it was a matter of saying to the Creator, "I need the opportunity to do it over again."

Nowadays the Sun Dance that I support and help to run is international; many people are allowed to dance, not just Lakota people. You might have as many as three hundred dancers at one Sun Dance, or, in a small community, as few as ten dancers. Before you actually start the dance, there are four days of purification. Four days of purification is teaching and praying and preparing for the dance, during which you don't have food or water—it's sort of like getting ready for the big race. It's a dance, so all the music and things have to be taught in the four days before the dance starts. The idea is for everyone to know what's going on during the dance. The dance itself goes on for four days. On each day you wake up at dawn and meet the sun as you go into what they call the dance harbor, and you dance the whole day until the sun goes down. Some people dance the whole night as well.

In the puberty ritual, the girl has to relate that she's having her period for the first time. What the tribe recognizes is her capacity to carry on life. The family helps by cherishing the young girl. It shows the tribe or the rest of the world that they do value this life that is now capable of bringing other life into the world. The whole family vows to feed the tribe and acknowledge the Creator, to say thank you and also in a sense to give the girl back to the creative process. The two rituals are singing the song for her and throwing out the ball as an affirmation of this young lady. The ball is just a symbol; it could even be a rubber ball. In the old days it was a leather pouch that was thrown into a ball; today, for all we know, you might use a basketball. The emphasis is not on the form, and the idea is to symbolize that the young lady has the world in her hands—that's what the ball symbolizes—and she throws it at her own whim and fancy. Women really do run the world today, and if they ever really and truly acknowledge that, we'd have a different world.

Everything is done through music in our tradition; music is our connection to the spirit world. The Western mind looks at the ritual and sees it as a power form. The Lakota mind and more natural religions look at music as the connection and experience of God. In our tradition music is expressed through using voice and drums, and the holy men are singers. When you're a composer and a keeper of traditional music, you're actually holy because all the rituals are dependent upon the music. Functionally we singers become the spiritual leaders. The words are important, but so is the vocal application to the note structure—what you would call harmonics. The lyrics are just words, and words don't have power unless they're related to something real, and that's what we call sacred language. To me if you harmonize through your voice or instrumentation, it removes obstacles and obstructions. The whole sense of frequency vibration you can achieve through music cuts through a lot of illusions. And when you can touch those tones that really are a harmonic in the universal order, that's a spiritual experience that creates, in a sense, the path of least resistance whereby the world and the universe return to order.

The purification lodge is a process whereby values are taught to individuals who willingly take part. In a ritual like this there's a physical cleansing and a spiritual cleansing. Hot rocks are brought into a lodge, and people literally sweat. What that does physically is bring all the toxins to the surface of a person's skin. It literally cleanses all the internal parts of the body. Spiritually, if you're putting yourself through this incredibly stressful experience, you have to pray a lot to get through it. So it puts a real emphasis on putting ego aside so that you can pray the correct way, where it's not such a physical test but a cleansing. This cleansing is a way of learning how to breathe.

Most Western systems have lost their connections to the spontaneous balancing of the physical forms and the spiritual forms. What these forms stressing the body do is acknowledge that the physical, organic connection to the world is breathing. If you learn how to breathe, it can slow the whole body down. Scientifically what happens when you slow the body down is the alpha waves in the brain start producing more alpha waves, and you may even touch theta, which is a really deep, contemplative, and peaceful state. If you bring the body to that level, all forms of aggression and emotionality go out the window.

What you experience is a real connection, a real attunement to your world. In most of the natural systems—such as Lakota and the Tao—that work on challenging the ego, the end result is to get to a real gentle state of mind of connecting with the world and with the Creator. When you learn how to breathe, it literally slows the body down. If you learn that breathing is the organic connection to the world, you would start learning how to breathe so that you would maintain a peaceful or a tranquil state of mind. If you *really* learn how to breathe, you would take better care of yourself, and your world wouldn't be so stressful.

Vision Quest is a process of finding yourself. New-Agers and a lot of other people have latched on to this idea of Vision Quest as a search for something outside of themselves, such as a vision, or God talking to them. And the presumption is that God is out there and can talk to you. But to the people who really do this, within our own culture and others who come to people like myself, the Vision Quest is simply a process of isolation that helps you find yourself, your own being. Of course the paradoxical intention is that if you find yourself, you'll also find God. This ritual differs from tribe to tribe. Within the Lakota tradition you vow to be isolated for anywhere from one to four days or four nights. Four days before you get into the ritual you stop having food and water. On the fourth day you have a little water to prepare for the rest of your vow, in which you go out into the hills and isolate yourself from your environment. The term *isolation* is really the wrong term, but we use it because you're isolating yourself from the people around you. But since the whole process is to come back to nature, it's not isolation, it's finding your own being. You do this quest whenever you have the need for it. You approach a medicine man or a holy man and say, "I need help." Preferably you would do it in the summer months, because it's a lot easier on the body. When you go out you don't have any clothes on other than one blanket and a peace pipe. You're isolated in one spot—which you're told you can leave at any time, but of course when you're told that, by pride you will stay there.

Among the Lakota traditions there's more value. It doesn't remove the human politics that occur in every religion or philosophy, but there's much more openness and honesty about the work and action. For me it wasn't so much a comparison or choosing the Lakota way; it just seemed the natural way to go. I haven't even wondered about how typical the Lakota tradition is of other Native American traditions because you simply do the role and function that you've been given by the people who come to you for help.

I'm into a comparative approach to spiritual development; I simply do what I need to do. I've always used some Christian analogies because I was raised as a Catholic. I went to church on Sundays and First Fridays and ceremonies because my grandma took me. But I was always in the Lakota way too. You might say I fell away from the Christian way when I went to prep school in Massachusetts. The practice, and what people's words were, were so different that it didn't appear to me a good way to be, so I simply fell away. But I don't take a position of "against" either. A lot of my work right now is working with different religions in the world. I do a lot of work with the National Council of Churches and the Buddhist community in America, and some of the Eastern religious adherents always end up finding me here in Taos. So my approach isn't an antireligion or an antiphilosophy; it's simply my choice to live this way. Because I see all these different religious forms, my awareness of them is just to help people make some understandings or make some transitions from one state of perception to a different perception that may help them arrive at their own inner truth.

At some point the people who chose religions and are really religious in their devotion to that form actually transcend it. That's because the spiritual experience is not a religious experience but a true connection to the Creator. And whatever you believe that Creator to be, you also transcend that. At some point you arrive at truth, where the religions and the forms of it fall away. I call this point "touching your own nature." If your nature truly is created by God, God is already within your nature. Once you touch that, you find that what people do is what shapes faith, but what people do also expresses, to a large extent, what they're going to be doing for the rest of their lives, and that spiritual experience allows you to cross obstructions or form differentiations to touch God in each other. The paradox is that the more each individual finds peace in his or her own heart, the more he or she will find it throughout the world. So religions and their principal tenets at some point fall away, to give way to the truth, to God's experience.

LAWRENCE KUSHNER

Lawrence Kushner has been rabbi of Congregation Beth-El in Sudbury, Massachusetts, since 1971. Under his leadership the congregation's 375 families have earned national prominence for their leadership and creativity. They translated, edited, and published the first gender-neutral Jewish prayer book. Rabbi Kushner originated the concept of the synagogue Havurot, small family fellowship groups, and has led more than fifty family Kalla weekends for personal religious growth. His books include Hasidic Interpretation of Scripture (1993); God Was in This Place and I Did Not Know (1992); and Honey from the Rock: Visions of Jewish Mystical Renewal (1977, 1990). He and his wife, Karen, have three children.

Prayer only sounds as if you're talking to God. In truth prayer is reciting the words of a script that has evolved and been evolving over the centuries and that gives form to the inchoate yearnings of your innermost being. For there's nothing new to say in prayer. Surely God has heard it all before. What you need to do in order to pray is to surrender your own expressions of gratitude and petition to the syntax of tradition. Only one who can allow the annulment of his or her self is capable of being transformed through the words of prayer or the lines of the great script. But as long as you cling to your discrete selfhood, you are unable to transcend yourself, and your prayers then go unanswered. For this reason the key to unlocking our most important songs is the script recorded in the prayer book.

Now, as with any good actor, occasional ad libs, inflectionary modification, and the rare forgetting of one's lines are part of the business. Even the sensation of improvisation does have its place, so long as you remember that your allegedly new creation has already been recited by the heavenly retinue since before the creation of the world. The script, in other words, is present whether or not the play is performed in the human prayer hall or in an act of solo meditation.

I personally pray through the words of the tradition. When I pray with the congregation, I recite the words in the liturgy. I don't lead the congregation, I just pray *with* the congregation where I'm a rabbi. How I pray is I walk into the room when services are called for, open the book, and do the best I can to read the prayers and mean them. I mean that in a very serious way. When the service is over, often nothing seems to have changed in me or in the universe, although sometimes it does. But the service invariably involves reading the words of that ancient script. There is very little in the nature of talking beyond that script. There's not much of what people would call creativity. Creativity comes from how I *read* the lines in the script: the inflections, the modifications, the number of times I'll recite the same line over again, the things I'll add to it. Prayer apart from that script in one sense is unimaginable, unintelligible, because that script exhausts everything there is and that needs to be said.

The script is the prayer book. It's been prayed for a couple of thousand years. It is the script that the Jewish people have evolved as the way to do their prayer business with the Holy One. I would imagine that other religious and spiritual traditions have their own prayer books, their own script. The fact that my script is Jewish is a coincidence of my birth. That's the way Jews talk to

God, but I have no doubt that if I were in another spiritual tradition, I'd talk to God in another language. But for me as a Jew, praying is the regular and routine recitation of those sacred words. It's become something like a chant, a self-transcending other mode of consciousness that I would hope to enter through the pious and routine and devout recitation of those words.

I wish I could say I enter that realm of consciousness regularly. The best I can come up with is, I do so not infrequently. There's a line from Dustin Hoffman in the movie *Little Big Man* that sums it up: "Sometimes the magic works, sometimes it doesn't. Okay, let's go have lunch."

During self-transcendence I don't froth at the mouth or glaze over or have light that leaks out of my facial apertures. I do have a heightened sense of my interdependence on all creation, of my place in it, and a hunch about the deep unity that joins everything to everything else. The word *mindless* is confusing, but during prayer there *is* something like mindlessness; that is, I'm not aware that it's me who's doing it. It's like when I'm dancing: I didn't know it was me who was dancing until the music stopped. But to say *mindless* also implies a sense of losing higher cognitive faculties. I think of prayer as something that goes beyond those faculties; it's the next step *after* serious thought.

Most discussions of prayer are based upon a model that says that God is utterly beyond people, other than people, and distant from people; the job of prayer is to somehow bridge the gap and reach to God. That language dismisses the way that probably 50 percent of the people in the universe pray—people like me who think of themselves as being within God, but just not able to understand it or to grasp it most of the time. For example, it's like I'm the wave and God is the ocean, and when I pray, I go, "Oh, my God! I'm part of the ocean!" And there's nothing that the wave has to tell the ocean, and the ocean already knows that. All I need to do is become aware of my real place in the order of being. That's the function of prayer: to remind me of that. There's a beautiful old teaching that comes in the name of Rabbi Kalonymos Kalmish Shapiro, of Piesetzma, who perished in the Warsaw Ghetto. He said, "Not only does God hear our prayers, God prays them through us as well." I become the words of my prayer and in doing that I make God's prayers my own. My goal in prayer is that my prayer should become the same as God's prayer. Then I'm no longer at odds with my life and my world and my universe. When my prayers are God's prayers, I am simpatico with it, I understand my place in it; "Oh, I see, this is the way it is supposed to be."

Thus the content of prayer is not real important. The script is essentially saying, "I am glad to be a human being and grateful to be able to utter these words and grateful for the people whom I love and who love me. I pray that I and everyone who does not understand why things are the way they are, or who is in pain because of that, will gain a greater sense of why things are the way they are and thereby have their pain diminish."

The basic rubric of all Jewish prayer is a *berakha*, or a blessing. It begins with the phrase "Praised are You, Lord our God, King of the universe who . . ." and then you fill in the blank. That, according to one tradition, might be recited with a different ending as many as a hundred times a day. There's a sequence of those blessings that one might recite on awakening, as part of the daily liturgy, or around events such as eating a meal. Each one of those blessings, those scripted prayer lines, are designed to have the effect of just momentarily helping us regain a heightened sense of awareness and gratitude and responsibility.

The one that I recite the most frequently, which, after having recited it ten thousand times, means much more than the simple words, is (translated from the Hebrew), "Holy One of blessing, Your presence fills creation. You bring forth this bread from the earth." I try to recite that before every meal. When it works, I all of a sudden realize, just for a second, "Oh, my God, I didn't make this food. I don't know how this food got here. I really am dumbfounded before the experience of my own sustenance, my own nourishment. I don't understand how it is that I'm able to stay alive."

Another blessing that I find myself reciting very often is the she-hekhi-yanu. It means "Holy One of blessings, Your presence fills creation. You have kept us alive and kept us together and got us to this sacred moment." So you would, by tradition, always recite it at the commencement of a festival or a great life passage. After a wedding the father of the groom might stand up and as part of a toast recite the she-hekhi-yanu. If you're in shape, you might recite it a dozen times a day, as in "it's so good to be alive, I'm so glad I'm alive."

There are specific blessings that you recite on seeing the first flower, on tasting fruit for the first time of the year, on hearing good news, on hearing bad news. The blessing on hearing bad news would be, "Holy One of blessings, Your presence fills creation. You are indeed the judge." I've always read it as a kind of pained resolution: *This is the way things must be.* It's officially recited on hearing the news that someone has died. There are also blessings over all kinds of food, blessings over celestial bodies.

I find a lot of comfort in the structure of the script. I like the parts of the prayer that I know so well that I can click onto autopilot. I've prayed them myriad times before, and I know them so well that they come out of my mouth as if they're my words. I can recite them literally without thinking, and that also is part of making something else happen.

After prayer, after having this heightened sense of reverence, you return to the community of people with a much more gentle appreciation for them. The only thing that would make you angry would be that you would also have a heightened sense of what you have to do to make the universe better. You always return from prayer in a way that makes it easier to hug the person next to you or look at them with a smile. It's not like you're blissed out; there's also a keen sense that you walk away with a sense of fire inside you, that you've got to go out and make the world better, that the reason the world is not as good as it could be is that you've been wasting your time on worthless things. In Judaism that's called *tikkun olam*; "repairing the creation." It ranges from apple-pie things, such as standing in a soup kitchen, to much more risky things, such as getting arrested or doing what has to be done to try to change the course of things.

Another metaphor for prayer would be that we can't live without water, but the only place to find drinkable water is in an underground stream deep beneath the surface, and it can only be drawn up to the surface with great effort and attention. Prayer is drawing that water to the surface to drink: you become refreshed and revitalized and go back to what you have to do with renewed enthusiasm.

NORMAN LEAR

Norman Lear—writer, producer, and director—is best known as the creator of "All in the Family" and other situation comedies—such as "Maude," "Sanford and Son," "Good Times," "The Jeffersons," "One Day at a Time," and "Mary Hartman, Mary Hartman"—that changed the face of American television in the 1970s. He is now head of Act III Communications, which owns seven independent television stations and a chain of independent movie theaters. Act III has produced the movies Stand by Me, The Princess Bride, *and* Fried Green Tomatoes. *In 1980 he became cofounder of People for the American Way, a constitutional-liberties organization.*

A few years ago I was invited to address more than ten thousand teachers at a convention of the National Education Association. I was cautioned not to imply anything that would conflict with my credentials as a civil libertarian and a First Amendment freak. But I thought, "Where is it written that civil libertarians and First Amendment advocates do not care about the spiritual condition of our species and our country?" I gave the speech, and it was well received. In part I said that all of humankind has been endowed with the capacity for awe, wonder, and mystery, the search for higher meaning, and the capacity to feel the rapture of being alive. That capacity comes to us genetically at birth. A culture that becomes a stranger to its own inner, human needs is a culture that has lost touch with the best in its humanity.

Czechoslovakian president Václav Havel has called for spirituality, moral responsibility, humaneness, and humility in politics, and most Americans would agree with that.

I asked church historian Martin Marty once, "Can you give me the shortest definition of worship?" He said, "Gratitude," and I've loved that definition ever since. But even more than that, it's the *awareness* of being in a state of gratitude. If you're feeling gratitude, you've got to feel gratitude in a direction. When that direction is outward, to me that's worship. I would submit the same definition for prayer. The object of the gratitude is to wish to be this much in touch all of the time. It would be impossible for us as humans, but the goal is to be in a perpetual state of gratitude.

I love the ceiling when I wake up in the morning. I could write a small book called *The Ceilings of My Life*. I remember the ceiling in our home as a boy; it was a little stucco ceiling that seemed close to my face while I was lying in bed. This seven foot room had a heating unit with a big brown stain around it, and I remember how unpleasant that was. And then I remember the first hotel that I stayed at where I looked at the ceiling and it was nice to look at. I've been aware of ceilings for all of my life from that point on. I have an enormous sense of gratitude when I look up at this ceiling here today. And when I've slept outdoors and the ceiling was the sky, well, what can I say? Now when I wake up in the middle of the night and turn over the pillow and move my knee out and find a cool spot in the sheets, it never happens without my attaching gratitude, it never happens without my saying, "My God, isn't this wonderful."

I have an abiding belief in the words of Emerson that say that we lie in the lap of an immense intelligence. I have an abiding belief in Lao-Tzu's words in the Tao, which expresses the same thought. We own none of our talents, and we own none of nature, quite obviously. We're here for a while and for that time they're there for us. Our talents and our intelligence pass through us, borrowed only temporarily from the universe.

I've found this piece of Talmudic wisdom within the past year. It started with "A man. . . ." Today it should be, "A person. . . ." A person should have a garment with two pockets. In the first pocket should be a piece of paper on which is written, "I am but dust and ashes." In the second pocket should be a piece of paper on which is written, "For me the world was created."

When I am really feeling that sense of appreciation, of gratitude, to the universe, to God, to nature, I am able to think, "Of course, for me. It's all created for me. It's all created for each of us." Once I chance upon that attitude, I can't force myself to feel otherwise because it's so commonsensically clear to me, that "Of course, it's here for me; what else is it here for?"

Then again, I can go through a day when I'm feeling nothing but sorrow for myself because something is on my mind and plaguing me. It may not be the least bit important, but I've lost all sense of that gratitude. When it returns, I think, "Oh, my God, I've got to make those spaces in between those feelings of gratitude shorter." And I think, as time goes by, I do; I'm more able to find that sense of appreciation.

When I look back in my work, I find in it evidence of the seeds of my spirituality. Throughout my life, when I meet people who knew me in high school, knew me in college, knew me in the service, knew me in the early years, I keep hearing anecdotes about myself that attach to me a deep spirituality that I had not been aware of. My mind hadn't considered myself as spiritual simply because I had not been thinking about those things. But when my wife, Lyn, and I met—almost nine years ago now—for the first time someone entered my life who was deeply and outwardly—not just inwardly—spiritual. She nourished this part of myself. I could discuss this part of me and learn about it for the first time. So I would say for the last eight years I've come to understand it better and to think about it.

Spirituality is in my work, it's in my life. Nadine Gordimer wrote, "For us the real definition of loneliness [is] to live without social responsibility." A year ago, People for the American Way issued a statement on spirituality and public service. We took a direct position— out of something that I initiated—that we couldn't allow respect for that transcendent journey to be owned by the fundamentalists, or the new-age swamis, or we people who are directly in the middle, or so-called Mainliners. *Everybody* owns it, and we mustn't cede that to any one group.

On my treadmill, every morning of my life, I have the Saint Francis of Assisi prayer, which, to me, says just about everything:

Lord, make me a channel of thy peace,
That where there is hatred, I may bring love;
That where there is wrong, I may bring the spirit of forgiveness;
That where there is discord, I may bring harmony;
That where there is error, I may bring truth;
That where there is doubt, I may bring faith;
That where there is despair, I may bring hope,
That where there are shadows, I may bring light;
That where there is sadness, I may bring joy.
Lord, grant that I may seek to comfort rather than to be comforted;
To understand than to be understood;
To love than to be loved.
For it is in giving that we are received,

It is by forgiving that we are forgiven,
And it is by dying that we awaken to eternal life.

Those are the best words I have found for prayer. What I love about it is it isn't asking for anything except to be a better person. It's the essence, I think, of what Jesus asked of his disciples and what the Buddha talks about. It seems to me the essence of everything. I would never consider praying to ask for anything, either for myself or for anybody else. All I can expect of it is to let me serve, to be the kind of person who can give as close to 100 percent of myself as I can.

Saint Francis's prayer is all about relationships. Let me bring love and forgiveness and harmony. And these words are the best prescription for living: "Grant that I may seek to comfort rather than to be comforted." It's happened that I've come back from a writer's meeting pretty unhappy; we didn't come up with anything new, and the script or the scene was in trouble, and I became deeply unhappy. And then suddenly, in the middle of the night or on the way home, I'll say, "Wait a second. I went into that meeting wishing to hear *from them* that everything was going to be okay, that they had the answers. I basically wanted to leave the meeting having been assured and convinced by my cohorts that everything was going to be okay. So, I was seeking to be comforted rather than to comfort others. When the prayer says, "By dying we awaken to eternal life," it isn't referring to literal death, but to the death of the self. Only when one dies in the self does one awaken to eternal life.

JOHN LEWIS

*John Lewis, one of the major leaders of the civil rights move-
ment, was first elected to represent Georgia's Fifth District in the
U.S. House of Representatives in 1986. A graduate of the
American Baptist Theological Seminary, Lewis was chairman of
the Student Nonviolent Coordinating Committee from 1963 to
1966. He was a leader of the march from Selma to Montgomery
that created pressure for passage of the Voting Rights Act in
1965. Lewis has a wife, Lillian, and a son, John-Miles.*

On the one hand prayer to me is an attempt to communicate with a power, with a force, with a being much
greater than I am. On the other hand it is a period of
simply having an executive session with yourself. It's a
period of being alone, a period of meditation, a period of
quiet and just being you.

It can happen in a public setting. It can happen in a
meeting. It can happen while you're flying in a plane or
riding in a car or waiting to make a speech or at almost
any time. You hear people from time to time say, "I need
to steal away and pray." In my own case I can steal away
almost anytime. I can be on the elevator. I can be involved in a march, a sit-in, some type of nonviolent protest, and still be engaged in prayer. And sometimes I pray
when I have something very difficult to deal with. You're
constantly in prayer to some spirit or some force to help
you make the right decision, to give you the courage to
follow through or to stand your ground.

I don't as a rule engage in formal prayer. When I first came to Congress, I attended the Thursday-morning prayer breakfast on a regular basis for the first two or three years. A conflict of meetings makes it impossible for me to go now. But that doesn't keep me from praying. When I go home in the evening, I pray just like when I was growing up. I don't necessarily get down on my knees and say a prayer before going to bed, but sometimes I'm in bed and I say a prayer. I'm always asking somebody, some force, some power—whether it's God Almighty or what I sometimes refer to as the Spirit of History—to take care of me, to help me make the right decision, to see me through something. Sometimes when I have a major statement to make on the floor, I call on that force, that source, to help me, to guide me.

I know that if it hadn't been for prayer, I wouldn't be where I am today. It's always been sort of a guiding force through the day. I actually don't know how many times during the day I pray. And it's not formal prayer, it's not saying, "O, Father" or "God Almighty." But I'm in constant prayer. Sometimes you can read something or hear something that suggests to you that you need to reach out to a source, to a power much greater than you are. And sometimes you get an answer, such as when you get the necessary encouragement or the necessary courage to do the right thing or say the right thing.

Sometimes prayer is just a quiet moment when you're not disturbed, when you can cite a saying from the Bible or even from English literature. Or it's when you reflect on something like the words from George Bernard Shaw that Bobby Kennedy used to quote all the time: "Some men see things that are and say why. I see things that should be and say why not." So often in speeches I will say things like "Our struggle is not a struggle that lasts for one day or one week or one month or one year. It is a struggle for a lifetime." I'll sit and think about that and reflect on it and meditate.

That's why prayer played such a major role in the civil rights movement for me. I did not feel the movement was just a social, political movement for civil rights. For me it was based on a deep religious conviction, and without prayer my involvement in the movement would have been like that of a bird without wings. You knew on a Freedom Ride that there was a possibility that you would not only be beaten and jailed but even killed. On Bloody Sunday—March 7, 1965—we attempted to march from Selma to Montgomery. We knew there was a possibility we would be arrested and jailed, and we also knew that we could be beaten. You had to be able to go on in spite of those possibilities—and that's what happened when the Sunday-afternoon state troopers said, "This is an unlawful march; you have three minutes to disperse and go back to your church." When they said that, we stopped and began passing the word back that we should kneel and pray. The troopers attacked us one and a half minutes later.

Prayer was a powerful instrument, a very powerful tool in helping not only to relieve some of the tension but in giving us the extra strength to go on, to continue. When I prayed, it was not just trying to communicate with God Almighty or with some supreme being or supreme force. We were also communicating and worshiping with others. It was like communicating with a band of angels and saints, a band of believers.

When I look back on my own life and what I've come through, I can say that it was the prayers of the true believers, the prayers of an involved community of similar minds, that made it possible for me to still be here. Sometimes when I look back at the film footage of that civil rights fight and see what happened to me at Selma or on the Freedom Rides, I have to believe that it was the prayer of the faithful that made it possible for some of us to still be here.

From time to time I feel the presence of that power, that force that I call the Spirit of History. Sometimes you're guided by it, led by it. Other times you're in tune with that force and you can communicate with it. You have to be in tune, and you have to allow yourself to be used by this Supreme Being. That's what made me feel when we were at the height of the civil rights movement—whether it was the march from Selma to Montgomery, or going on the Freedom Rides—that we were involved in something like a Holy Crusade. It was an extension of my religious convictions, of my faith. We would sing a song or say a prayer, and it was an affirmation that it was the right thing to do. At that time we were communicating with a Supreme Being, with this force.

Prayer is one of the most powerful—well, I don't want to call it a weapon, but it's a tool, an instrument, a way of reaching out that humankind has. We can and do use it to deal with problems and the things and issues that we don't understand, that we don't quite comprehend. It's very hard to separate the essence of prayer and faith. We pray because we believe that praying can make what we believe, our dreams and our visions, come true.

MARTIN E. MARTY

Martin E. Marty, a Lutheran minister, is Fairfax M. Cone Distinguished Service Professor of the History of Modern Christianity at the University of Chicago Divinity School and senior editor of Christian Century. *He is president of the Park Ridge Center for the Study of Health, Faith, and Ethics. Marty has written more than forty books, including* Righteous Empire, *which won the National Book Award in 1972. He directs the Fundamentalism Project, an international public policy study of the American Academy of Arts and Sciences, and co-edited* Fundamentalism Observed *(1991),* Fundamentalisms and Society *(1993), and* Fundamentalisms and the State *(1993) with R. Scott Appleby. Marty is currently completing the third volume in a four-volume history of American religion. He and his wife, Harriet, live in Riverside, Illinois. They have five children, two foster children, and eight grandchildren.*

I don't think I've ever been asked to define prayer, so I'll make up a definition on the spot. The most immediate thing that comes to my mind would include some use of the word *conversation*, recalling the fact that the context for the word *conversation* allows for both "talk" and "way of life." You may argue with God—"Why are you doing this?" "Give me a fair shake," or "Reveal yourself"—and you may even give Him an examination—"I will put the Lord to a test." But prayer as conversation is neither of those. Conversation's distinctive character is that you never know where it will go. If you conceive of prayer as being in that mode, you turn the next page in a book on spiritual development and find a marvelous, surprising insight. The King James Version of the Bible says, "May your conversation be godly." Prayer is also a conversation with the Thou (with a capital *T*), a conversation that takes the shape of words spoken or unspoken or a way of life that expresses confidence in the relationship.

I start my own day invariably—and this is what Lutherans are supposed to do, though not many do—by making the sign of the cross on my body as a token of my baptism. In our faith-understanding (Rom. 6), "You are buried with Christ and risen." That form of prayer is to betoken the fact that whatever guilt I have from yesterday is gone. I'm gone. Yesterday does not exist. The only way it exists is in the mental attitudes we have today. The act reminds me that I cannot do anything about yesterday; I can only do things about today and I only have strength for today. So that's a gesture, the only one that I make consistently. This signal of nonverbal prayer carries me through the day.

Altogether I use five types of prayer. First I pray every morning at 5:59 A.M. I go back into the bedroom, having been up an hour, and I read the Moravian *Losungen* for my wife and myself. This is the 263rd year of the Moravian daily text. This book helped inspire John Wesley, the father of Methodism, and it's the book that the anti-Nazi German theologian Dietrich Bonhoeffer used in his subversive seminary. Each page presents two Scripture verses that Moravian elders chose by lot plus two hymn verses and then a little prayer adapted to it. The fact that the elders draw them by lot helps you encounter a range of things that wouldn't occur otherwise. You might be down some day and they present "up" passages, or you might be cocky some day and they offer humbling passages; there's a serendipity to them.

A second mode is that I am often in a situation that

amounts to the equivalent of prayer. I live a half hour
from my work, and travel time is the only time I'm
alone. Now and then I'll play National Public Radio, but
more often than not I'll just turn on a classical-music
station and indulge in a kind of a reverie. Twelve years
ago, when my first wife was terminally ill, I moved my
study into her bedroom. For those nine months I never
once left during any evening or for any trip away. But I
would teach each morning very early. During that year
I would begin the day feeling myself to be in an almost
impenetrable darkness of soul. That probably was good,
because it helped me be in some empathy with my wife;
she had a more existential engagement with suffering, although we both foresaw terrible losses. So I would have
all that in mind. Just as most people, the first few minutes after they wake up, experience darkness, I would
have that feeling. Then I would swing out onto the expressway, put the music on, and rather systematically focus on a few biblical words about prayer. They reminded
me to take no thought for the morrow, to have no anxiety or guilt, but to focus on the present day. If a thought
about tomorrow would cross my mind, I would recall that
I was never promised that I'd have strength for tomorrow; I *was* promised that I would be visited today. What
was bugging me was an ill-defined someday which inev-
itably would come, did come, and has gone. When the
day came, my wife and I had the strength to accept it. To
engage in that kind of focused, steadfast, driven kind of
thing while being on the expressway and joining the
flow of traffic represents a second mode for me.

Third, I do little stabs at prayer. Something just
crosses your mind if you are in a certain stance. I'm not
a very good pray-er. What I mainly do is pray in the
community. I try to be in church every Sunday. While
the Eucharist is *the* big deal—for me it is a prayerful act,

as I join in the company of those who have gone before and will come—and while the message of the Good News is meaningful, I have to say that for me as high a point in the service as any is the act of intercessory prayer, to me the highest mode of prayer. Intercession is that part of the service when you pray for other people. The Lutheran concept of the priesthood of all believers really had its breakthrough in this concept of intercessory prayer. We are all priests in that we are all equal in our freedom and ability to pray for each other in this highest act.

Presbyterian theologian William May says there are three elements in any fulfilled intercessory prayer. On the one hand there's a bidding—sometimes it begins with silence, sometimes you bring your own need. Our church bulletin will have a list of twenty or thirty people. I know that this man's been laid up with multiple sclerosis and this one has cancer of the tongue and this one had a heart bypass. In good intercessory prayer someone can stand up and say, "My sister has terminal cancer; you may not know her, for she lives in Iowa, but I want you to . . ." No need of the gathered assembly is too trivial, too intimate, to be brought to God's and the company's attention.

The second thing that good intercessory prayer does is to help the congregation discover those who would otherwise be overlooked. Good intercessory prayer bids you each week to picture the homeless, the Somalian children, the Bosnians, and the ghetto. Obviously this has to be symbolic because you can't do a global tour each week, and you can't even canvas your own city entirely. But lifting these images up commits you to a way of life. If you find it important to commend them to the community's and God's attention, then you have a different relationship to them than you otherwise would.

Third, in the Christian orbit, intercessory prayer must *always* include the enemy. That enemy could be of all kinds. It could be represented by another faction in the congregation, the spouse at the moment, Saddam Hussein, political opponents, David Koresh, any enemy of the good. You have a different relationship to each if you hold them in your intercessory prayer. So this becomes the kind of prayer that helps make us part of the worldwide community as well as the intimate local community.

A fourth form of prayer is what I call prayerful reading. I decided that I'm not a good meditator; I do not have the kind of brain for abstraction or "centering" that says I should seek a void, that I should, in classical language, stare at God face-to-face and seek the vision of God. I don't seek any of that. In our tradition you don't aspire to see the face of God; in Exodus we learned we'd be annihilated if we did. God is hidden. God comes to us in the wounds of Jesus and the tracks of the prophets in history, in the saints and martyrs, in the household names and in the ordinary people. All we know about God is what we get through the funny little tracings and tracks in history. So I want to pray, converse, communicate, through those historical modes. Meditation doesn't do it for me. What I do therefore—it's kind of a crasssounding term—is "hitchhike." I hitchhike using the vehicles, the instruments, of people who are better at devotion than I am. I'm not someone who could write like Mozart or who could play Mozart, but I am ennobled when I listen to Mozart or read his scores. I'm not a prayerful genius like the religious philosopher and scientist Pascal. I am not even someone who could edit and expound Pascal. But I can read him prayerfully, and the thoughts he inspires will convey me to different levels of being, to new depths. So I spend a lot of time with anthologies of prayer, with quotations, sourcebooks, the Paulist series on spirituality, and so on. Whether all those trips produce the language of "I" and "Thou" I'm not sure, but I am a book person, and therefore if I draw close to God, it is likely to be through reading.

At the University of Chicago I have an office next door to David Tracy, a Catholic theologian. Tracy and Machiavelli have taught me that you converse with books. Machiavelli says that before he goes into his library, he takes off muddy, dusty clothes and puts on garments "regal and courtly," because for the next four hours he's going to converse with the generous, great people of all ages. They will share with him, and he will learn from them. I sacralize what he is talking about secularly and say that's what I do when I converse with these texts by Juliana of Norwich and Margery Kempe and Jon van Ruysbroeck and so on. You *can* converse with your library. You never know where the great souls of the past will take you. To the pure pray-ers this would mean that my experience is kind of a second-hand experience. I admit it is; I'm limited to it, but I don't mind it. It is sustaining and effective.

An essay that taught me much about prayer at a time when I was stuck was by theologian Donald Capps, of Princeton. He takes up the issue of the "Thy will be done" prayer. That has always given me trouble, for "Thy will be done" sounds like resignation and nothing but that. While acceptance of the divine will is a positive, open act, resignation is a negative, defeating act. Whenever you say, "Not my will, but thine be done . . ." it sounds like, "Well, God, we're having a contest, and you win. You're bigger than I am, and you're smarter than I am, and you've got a stronger will than I have. I tried to bend it, but I couldn't, so good-bye. I wish it had turned out otherwise, but your will be done because you're

God." Capps says we need to notice two of the Gospels that both have Jesus praying in Gethsemene. Jesus tells God the Father, "Thy will be done"—and then *he goes on praying*; he goes on with the conversation. "Thy will be done" is not the last word.

Capps brings to mind a comparable relationship of a good child and a good parent who are in conversation with each other. Because they are in conversation, they have some sense of the range of each other's expectations. If the child were to come along and say, "I want a skateboard," and the parents were to say, "They're too dangerous," then the child starts the long process of showing his competencies and the parents might show their generosity of spirit. Or you ask for a bicycle or something like that that you know is in range, and they say, "You haven't been a good boy this year; how about tidying up the act a little bit?" and you say, "But look how responsible I've been with my paper route." You then converse, you negotiate. The main thing is, *you don't break off the conversation*. And the odds are, you *might* get that skateboard or bike. If you don't, you may have disappointment, but not resignation, for you never break off the conversation.

The other corollary of the conversational metaphor, the other thing that has been most helpful for learning the life of prayer, was an image I got from a book by Arthur Frank, *At the Will of the Body*. Frank is a Calgary, Alberta, medical anthropologist who at age forty got cancer. His book is just a marvelous reflection on illness, a book written at the edges of faith and nonfaith, of piety and nonpiety. Reading the book, you couldn't tell whether Frank is a believer or not, but he helps those who believe.

He said that during chemotherapy he had, across the room from him, a poster of Chagall's *Jacob Wrestling with the Angel*. Yet we don't really know with whom Jacob is wrestling: Is it God? Is it an angel? Is it another human being? Is it a vision? Is it a fantasy? Frank speculates that "good" Jacob is wrestling with the other side of Jacob, who was not a very nice man. In the midst of this contest this Other wants to be released to go on his way because neither is prevailing, and Jacob says, "I will not let you go unless you bless me." Then the Other touches Jacob in the thigh and wounds that sinew—Genesis says that to this day Jews do not eat of that sinew—and he gets the blessing. Frank used that as a metaphor that I convert into a metaphor for prayer: *Prayer never takes you out of the world of struggle*. It might take you out of the world of fights in which God is always going to win or death is always going to win, but it doesn't take you out of the world of struggle. There's no meaningful blessing without the wound, and there need be no wound that is not capped by blessing. The two are simply knotted together the way Jacob and Esau were in the womb. I found that to be a very useful image for the life of prayer. Most prayer as I would pray it at 5:59 in the morning or in church is not that vehement struggle. But when the rough times come, believers would have that general conversation going and you move from the parent-child or friend-friend or husband-and-wife image that Capps uses into the language of struggle, this dialectic, this yin-and-yang, this intertwining of the wound and the blessing.

Finally, my last form of prayer is that I sometimes ask God for things as part of the conversation that goes on all the time, just as I will ask my wife for some things, and she will ask me. But when my first wife was utterly ridden with cancer cells, emaciated and all, I wouldn't have dreamed of asking, "Oh, God, reverse these cells and give me a healthy-bodied spouse again." That was simply out of the range of this mode of conversation. What she and I prayed for was that love would be stronger than death, that nothing would separate us from the love of God, that we would be given strength for the day when it came—and when it came, we had it. We played Brahms's *Requiem* and a lot of the Bach masses and passions for the last hours as she went into coma. The records were all forms of prayer. Through it all she and I and our sons were asking for strength. But I'm not much of a believer in what most people call miracles.

With the Koran I believe that medicine is the miracle. Our God is essentially hidden, mysterious, steadfast, and compassionate, but not reducible to my expectations. He does not finally abandon us, but weeps with us, identifies with us, sympathizes with us. When I ask for things, I ask to be part of that empathy, sympathy, steadfastness; I don't ask God to "Give me a raise" or "Give me a fancy car." I might, as a natural human being, erupt now and then in such a thing, but I've never seen prayer as that kind of magic transaction.

I find the most offensive kind of prayer to be when 250 Marines get killed in Lebanon and four survive and the survivors' families go on television and say, "Well, we really prayed, so they were spared." That's an unbiblical game; it's based on magic, superstition. I like the matter-of-factness of Jesus when they asked him about the man born blind; Jesus says, "Did he sin or did his parents, you ask me? He was born blind. Things just happen." *It rains on the just and the unjust alike.* So you don't hear about this kind of magic from people who are in regular conversation with God; you hear it most from people who think they've got God figured out. They had been very remote and then they phase into prayer on their lucky day; they win the lottery. Then they say, "I prayed about these bills and God gave money to me." No, God didn't give you anything, God didn't rig that lottery, *it just happened*. To me theology and prayer are what we do with what just happened, what interpretation we put on the happenings, and what attitudes we have toward them.

Awe is an important part. The purpose in bowing the head or folding the hands or kneeling in worship, in praise, or opening the hands up to the heavens, or in being apparently "reduced" is not to say that as a human being I am and will be nothing but totally depraved. Instead it signals that in that encounter with the Thou that is the one beyond all other beyonds and greater than all greatests, I am moved to shudder a little bit, to stand on holy ground and take my shoes off. All the Bible pictures in my Sunday-school leaflets showed the shepherds at Christmas, the prophets confronting the whirlwind, putting their robed arm up in front of their eyes. One is in awe, and it's a step toward shedding our claustrophobia-inducing egocentrism. Philosopher Jerome Miller says that this awe we find in prayer frees us from that. It breaks open that tight chamber of self, those elements of me that I must leave behind: my pride, my achievements, my arrogance, my SOB-ism. I can leave them now without regret or mourning, because I'm freed by this act of expressing awe. That's why prayer and worship are finally celebrative. That's even true after you leave a funeral, where you've been praying Psalm 90, the standard burial Psalm. Very often you stop on the way home to have some beer and cold cuts; you toast the past and future, you joke a little bit about Grandpa. The act of prayer isn't finished without evidence of an openness toward celebration. I'm not saying that people in concentration camps should make a toast; I'm saying that the normal acts of worship that reduce us before a Greater Being are not to put us under the power of God as dominator, a cruel, capricious master, a patriarch, but to free us from that bondage in which we live.

On my door I have a picture of Pogo that says, "We have faults we've hardly used yet." And under that I have one from Reinhold Niebuhr. It's not a prayer but it's a trigger for prayer: "Nothing that is worth doing can be achieved in our lifetime, therefore we must be saved by hope. Nothing which is true or beautiful or good makes complete sense in any immediate context of history, therefore we must be saved by faith. Nothing we do, however virtuous, can be accomplished alone, therefore we are saved by love. No virtuous act is quite as virtuous from the standpoint of our friend or foe as it is from our standpoint, therefore we must be saved by the final form of love which is forgiveness." I use lines like that and build my prayers out of them.

CAROLE MU'MIN

Carole Mu'min, a businesswoman and community activist in Washington, D.C., served in the communications offices of the Kennedy, Johnson, and Carter administrations. She now runs an administrative support and training company, is active in a variety of low-income programs, and founded People in Service to Others (PISTO). A member of Masjid Muhammad in Washington, she is active in the Interfaith Conference of Greater Washington. She and her husband, Ibrahim Mu'min, who is cochair of the Washington office of the National Conference (founded as the National Conference of Christians and Jews), have four children and seven grandchildren.

I define prayer by the word *contact*. Real prayer is making that contact with the infinite Creator of the universe. I've come to understand that the essence of prayer is not just the words but the actual connecting. Let's say you say the Lord's Prayer. It has meaning, but they're words. The difference is that praying with contact means that you know that there's somebody there on the other side, you know that God is there. You absolutely know the existence of the Creator. It's like an electrical charge; it's not just space or air. There's a connection between you and your Creator.

Being Muslim, by obligation we have to make our five prayers a day. The reason I want to highlight that is that I don't make contact every time I pray. The prayers are obligatory and regular, but, for whatever reason, sometimes your mind is wandering, and you don't always make the contact. So you do the prayers because you're obligated to.

We have *Fajr* prayer in the morning; that usually occurs sometime around five or six A.M. Then we have *Thuhr* prayer, which is in the afternoon—usually around twelve or one o'clock. Then you have the *Asr* prayer. You also have *Maghrib*, a late-afternoon prayer that you say after the sunset. Then you have the evening prayer, *Asha*, that's usually about nine-thirty or ten P.M.

The prayers are not really lengthy. The *Fajr* prayer is the shortest prayer; you only have to do two *rakahs*. *Rakahs* are the movements in Muslim prayer: standing, bending, kneeling, head on the floor. To complete one *rakah* would be to stand, to bend, to kneel, to put your head on the floor, and then get back up again. For the noon prayer and the afternoon prayer and the prayer that's late at night, you do four *rakahs*. For the prayer that comes right after sunset, we do three *rakahs*. The *Fajr* takes about five minutes. In the afternoon, however, it takes close to ten minutes to pray.

There's a ritual, set prayer during these times. With every prayer, we say,

In the name of God, most gracious, most merciful.
Praise be to God, the Cherisher and Sustainer of all the worlds,
Most gracious, Most merciful,
Master of the day of judgment,
Thee do we worship and Thine aid we seek,
Show us the straight way,
The way of those on whom Thou has bestowed thy grace,
Those whose fortune is not wrath,
And who go not astray.

Every *rakah* begins with that prayer, and it's the most often-said prayer in Islam. It's called the *Alfatiha*, or the opening.

All of the prayers are made up of chapters or verses from the Koran. The other prayers differ because you can pick and choose the ones that you like as long as they make up one complete *ayet*, or one complete paragraph. One would be, "To Thee have we granted the fount of abundance, so turn to your Lord in prayer and sacrifice." That's one of my favorites.

As I've matured in my faith and in my life, I connect more often now. When I'm getting ready to come to prayer, I'm much more aware of what is about to happen besides the fact that I'm getting ready to say some words or repeat a poem or a story or something like that. What I'm actually doing is fulfilling an obligation. For prayer is not something *we* made up; it's been requested through all of the faiths. That's how the Lord's Prayer came about; *God* asked that we pray to Him. As we mature, as we study our faith and get more understanding, the meanings of these things become deeper to us. That meaning makes the attitude different. Sometimes when I get ready to begin prayer, I can't even pray because the reality of what is about to happen is so overwhelming, I just kind of cry; I am that filled up.

But there was a time when I didn't even know that I could connect; I just prayed. As children we go to bed, we say our prayers at night or whenever it is, and it doesn't occur to us that there's any connection. We're talking, we say our prayers, and that's it. For me that was all I did for a long time. Prayer was just a natural way of life. But what eventually would come to my understanding would be the contact or the fact that there was another layer or level to what this prayer was all about. I think that such knowledge comes from studying your faith, which means that you're learning more about your Creator and the awesomeness of this whole reality. The day came when it was like a light bulb coming on—you know you're praying because God *asked* you to pray, told you to pray. All along I thought I was praying because *I* wanted to pray, but the reality is that we pray because God has asked us to pray. When I realized that, it was like, "My God, this is really awesome. Let me listen to what God has asked me to do." As you think about it, and go deeper and deeper into it and get more reality, all of a sudden you're standing in the midst of prayer and you realize what it all means.

Now, how does prayer affect everyday life? I have a business and a family and a husband and children and grandchildren and things like that, and so there are times when I'm pulling myself out of what is very consuming, and therefore I'm not really tuned in to the prayer. But it's obligatory, and God knows that we are not perfect, so that even though I don't feel like I'm connecting, at least I'm fulfilling my obligation, and maybe somewhere along that line God will show His mercy on me.

I'm fortunate in that my husband is also a praying man. Early on in our marriage, when we wouldn't see eye to eye, he would be the one who would say, "Let's say a prayer over this." Now, there you are, in the middle of a healthy discussion (as we call them!) when suddenly you stop and pray for guidance: I attribute *that* to why our marriage is together today. When you come up out of prayer, it puts everything in perspective. I certainly agree with those who say, "A family that prays together stays together." Even though you might have been as mad as you could have been at the time, once you finish praying, you just have to realize that you must put things in perspective and recognize that the most important thing is what *God* wants you to do. It wasn't that every time we finished prayer, I necessarily agreed with my husband, but it helped in terms of how we handled our differences.

I think that goes across the board. No matter what is going on in my life, if I can just have the wherewithal to pull myself out and go into prayer, the relief that I get from praying—I don't care *what* the problem is—is immense. Prayer is turning the problem into God's hands; I have to give it up. Whatever it is that's too heavy for me to handle, I have to give it up, and I think that's the value of prayer: the recognition of someone who is really capable of handling every situation and taking control of every affair and getting you together—getting you straightened out or giving you the help that you need. So there's no question: anytime I go into prayer, I come out a better person. Period.

Sometimes I almost "pray without ceasing," as they say, because I can't make it by myself, without God's help. I am in constant remembrance, and I'm forced to be in constant remembrance because I'm in so much need all the time. You have family, you have community life, you have business life; there's so many things going on. You're either in prayer of thanksgiving or in prayer of asking. Sometimes you just want to say, "Thank you, I know I'm fortunate." There are so many times when I'm thanking, but still I need this and I need that. I really know that God can perform and fulfill any need that I have.

I also understand prayer goes hand in hand with work. In Islam you don't pray and just sit there—although as merciful as the Creator is that I've known, there are times when I just sit down and get the blessing anyway. But as Muslims we are taught prayer and good works. You are supposed to pray and then you're supposed to do the best you can. And with that best you're supposed to know that God is aware of your best and will handle the affair after that. There are some things that are bigger than you and I can handle, that we just can't figure out.

I pray for protection, for guidance—for everything. I
feel as though I'm in constant prayer. When I'm walking
down the street, I'm praying. I make a lot of mistakes, so
I'm praying all the time for God to have mercy on me
and to help me deal with myself in terms of my short-
comings. I'm in prayer on a constant basis, and in constant remembrance.

Have I received answers to prayers? Oh, my goodness,
yes. There are times when I get answers before I can
even get the request out. How can I tell? In my lifetime
I've had a couple of very, very, soul-searching encounters
where I've actually heard a voice. Now, I'm not so sure
it was outside of me—I don't want to get spooky—but it
happened two times in my life when I was under extreme
pressure. It certainly was profound, and it's probably
somewhat responsible for my becoming a Muslim. But I
normally feel the prayer is answered because I see the
manifestation; I ask for something and then it will happen. Patience is critical, and I guess we're all working on
that. But there's not much in terms of what I've asked
for that hasn't been answered, to be honest about it. I
could give you a material example, but it would not be
any more rewarding than having a child graduate from
college or just graduate from high school. I asked God to
protect my children and grandchildren, and they have
been well protected and they're doing well and I'm glad.

There was a time when I wanted a wall up in my
house and didn't have the money, and out of the blue I
got the wall. I wanted to build another room in my base-
ment area because my husband has a very large family.
They like to come back and forth and I enjoy them
when they come. One of the things that was missing was
a multipurpose room that could also serve as an extra
bedroom. It was something that I wanted, but there were
other things that took up the money, and I just couldn't

seem to get it. So I just asked God to let me be successful in getting the wall up. About a year later I was talking with my brother, and he said, "I'll put your wall up as a gift." It took him about a year, but the wall is up. People come and say, "Oh, this is a beautiful wall," for it's not just a wall but has bookshelves and a beautiful door in it. So, I asked for it, then left it alone, and eventually it happened. I don't think there's anything that doesn't happen just about every day. Maybe that's why I'm in constant remembrance, because I'm also in constant thankfulness for the things that I'm receiving. I've got sense enough to know that they are gifts from God, and I appreciate them. I would like for them to continue, so I'm constantly thanking.

One of the most beautiful things that I've ever seen in my life was when I went to *Haj* in 1978 to Mecca. I can remember going into Medina, having arrived in the airport in Saudi Arabia, and when I stepped out on the balcony, there was a call to prayer at the time. The land is flat, so you can see for great distances, and as far as the eye could see, the whole country was in prayer. Everyplace that I could see, people were doing the rituals for Muslim prayer. It was absolutely beautiful. I enjoy the *Jummah* prayers on Friday where we have congregational prayer. We line up together and bow down together. There's no color, no racism in Islam, so the person next to you could be short or tall, fat or skinny, black or white, poor or rich; it doesn't make any difference. It is so beautiful when people stand together like that. Neither age nor financial situation matter when you go down in prayer to Allah.

We have congregational prayer at home with my husband and the family and our friends. It's a beautiful thing to pray together. I enjoy it when I go to interfaith conferences and events where we have interfaith prayer; I get just as emotional then. Prayer in every language is beautiful. We have family members who are Baptists, Catholics. You can enjoy the beauty of God any way it's expressed. "Ooh, let me see how you worship? It's just beautiful." "Ooh, look at the way the Jews do it, isn't this just lovely, I love this." "Look at the way the Catholics do it; that's fine too." Was I always able to do that? No. Why wasn't I always able to do it? Because I had been taught to be very dogmatic. Life taught me better. Sometimes I think people are afraid they might be converted if they enjoy someone else's things. I'm just very fortunate in that my husband and I are both strong in our Islamic faith, and I think that is why we can enjoy other folks' faith so much. Instead of any kind of fear we see the beauty. One of the things that makes this country so great is that all the religions have the freedom to worship. I can enjoy the many ways that people worship in America because I know there's only one God.

RONALD Y. NAKASONE

*Ronald Yukio Nakasone, an ordained Jodoshinshu (Pure Land)
Buddhist priest, is on the doctoral faculty of the Graduate Theological Union and the Institute of Buddhist Studies in Berkeley,
California, where he teaches Buddhist philosophy, ethics, and
aesthetics. He is particularly interested in bioethical issues and
the needs of the elderly. He is the author of* Ethics of Enlightenment: Sermons and Essays in Search of a Buddhist Ethic
*(1990). A native of Hawaii, he is an accomplished calligrapher
and a skilled practitioner of kendo (Japanese fencing). He and
his family live in Fremont, California.*

As Buddhists we really do not have prayer if prayer is defined to be solicitation or evocation of divine favors. We
do not pray to anyone or anything. Buddhists have the
Buddha of course, who can be interpreted in any number
of ways. But generally speaking, Buddhists believe that
Sakyamuni (ca. 563–463 B.C.E.), the historical Buddha,
and even the celestial Buddhas, symbolize and synthesize
the highest ideals and aspirations that we have as human
beings. We Buddhists are optimists. We believe that humanity is intrinsically good, pure, and replete with virtues. Compassion is the greatest virtue.

In lieu of prayer all Buddhists practice some kind of
meditation. Some, of course, engage in meditation more
seriously than others. Meditation is mindfulness. Mindfulness in its ultimate sense means to be fully aware of
the reality of the world and the human condition. It

means to see that all things and all beings are mutually related and interdependent. Sakyamuni realized his truth and became the Buddha, "The Enlightened One." The goal of all Buddhists is to attain the same realization as Sakyamuni. All beings are to become the Buddha.

Enlightenment is achieved when the mind is calmed and ultimately stilled. When the mind is undisturbed, when the mind becomes mirrorlike, we are able to apprehend all things without prejudice, with equanimity, and with absolute clarity. The mirrorlike mind allows us to apprehend true reality. More importantly, enlightenment allows us to perceive the sufferings of others, feel their sufferings, and move to relieve them.

When we enter into meditation, we resonate to the rhythm of forces that we believe to be greater than ourselves. These forces that resonate within us and throughout the universe support us and give meaning to our lives. The Buddhists call this the *Dharma*, or Truth. The realization of this Dharma is spiritually transforming. It breaks our self-centeredness, because we come to understand that we are part of a greater reality and that we live in an interdependent world. This spiritual transformation quickens two virtues: wisdom and compassion. Wisdom means simply to see things as they really are, to see things in their purity, to see things in the interdependence of their relationships, to see things in their absolute quiescence. The corollary to wisdom is compassion. Compassion is to identify with the suffering of others, to make their suffering ours, and to move to remove their sufferings.

There is a third virtue, which in actuality is probably more important than wisdom and compassion. We call this virtue *upaya*, or "skill-in-means." *Upaya* is the implementation of wisdom in concrete and compassionate action. Wisdom gives us the ability to know how much to help, how not to help, and when to help. Wisdom and compassion are acted out in *upaya*. *Upaya* is a very profound virtue in Buddhism.

Meditation is done every day. Mindfulness should be practiced daily. Some people practice meditation more rigorously than others. Some people enter into prolonged periods of regular meditation. Others may do it when they have a quiet moment to calm the mind and enter into reflection. Quiet fills the mind and the self.

In a sense, meditation is withdrawing from the world. But by withdrawing from the world we are able to fortify ourselves to face it with confidence and vision and purpose. Based on this experience, on introspection and calming, we are thus better able to go out and meet the challenges of the world and engage ourselves in the work of relieving the suffering of others.

Some Buddhists enter into mindfulness through Buddhist chants. Chanting is nothing more than the recitation of the Buddhist sutra, the Buddhist documents that are the direct words of the Buddha. By chanting the sutra we hear the teachings of the Buddha once more, again and for the first time. Chanting focuses the mind, stills the emotions. The mind therefore becomes mindful of the Buddha and his virtues and his teachings. In both of these—meditation and chanting—we become more receptive to forces that guide us and support us. In so doing, as we calm our minds, we are able to see people and things with more heartfelt objectivity.

Chanting for Buddhists is done at home. We do not only go to the temple to do this. Most Buddhists have a little personal or family shrine at home. The observance or meditation is done every morning. As soon as we are awake, we greet the Buddha. Every evening we bid the Buddha good night. This is a very important function in our spiritual lives because it means the Buddhist religion is not separate from ourselves, or from our homes, or from our families. We do not have to go to church or temple to commune with the Buddha. We have no special day that is important. Every day is a good day, every day is a special day, every day deserves mindfulness and appreciation. Every day also gives us an opportunity to work out our karmic destiny and is an opportunity to develop our spiritual lives.

Normally, in the Japanese Buddhist tradition, our chants are in Sino-Japanese—Chinese writing with Japanese pronunciation. These chants, because we've done them for so many years, have a soothing effect, a quieting effect. Tradition is very important to us, so we chant every day. I try to do it at least once a day in the morning for about ten minutes. Care of the shrine is also important: making sure the shrine is clean, making sure there are fresh flowers. Normally there's an image of the Buddha there; that's essential. We have offerings by means of flowers, candles, and incense. These three are fundamental. Sometimes we offer fruit or things of that nature to the Buddha. Oftentimes we report to the Buddha when something wonderful happens. We articulate this in front of the shrine. Next to the shrine would be reminders of our ancestors, and we sort of report to them about some of the accomplishments we may have done today, or some of the sad things that may have happened.

Recently I lost my mother, and usually in Buddhist homes we place a picture or some kind of a reminder of the deceased next to the shrine. Near our shrine we have pictures of my mother and my father-in-law and my grandfather. When we greet the shrine of the Buddha every morning and every evening, it reminds us of our past. It serves to instill a sense of gratitude for the people who have gone before us and for their sacrifices. It reaffirms our ties with our family and with our community.

Life passes on, and we must establish that somehow we are products of the larger rhythm of life that will continue. When I die, I will live on in the memories of my children and hopefully in their work.

When my mother passed away, the first thing I did was go to my family shrine and offer all the things that needed to be offered to the Buddha and to chant. This had a way of centering me, of calming me, and, in a sense, of putting things in perspective. It's also a time for personal reflection, and a time to fortify family unity. Because my wife and my daughter were there, we honored the moment with a short service. This was a way to remember my mother, to remember ourselves as a family and our connections to her, our humanity, and our relations to the Buddha.

The Japanese Buddhists have an elaborate memorial ritual. We have an elaborate funeral service and what we call memorial observances every seven days. We used to do this in the past—we don't do this too often now—and it happened every seventh day until the forty-ninth day, seven services in all. When I was a priest, I found this to be very helpful, especially the forty-ninth-day service, the last service, because usually about this time, which is five or six weeks after the funeral, people get very depressed because they are no longer busy making arrangements for the funeral or sending out thank-you notes. Others don't call or come anymore to visit them. Somehow life goes on, but at this time people tend to be very depressed because they have time to themselves, time to reflect and time to think about what has happened. The forty-ninth-day service is usually a large service, an important service. Usually the family all comes together with very close friends. It's a time to remember, a time to reaffirm family ties, and a time to honor the deceased.

Buddhists also have annual memorial services. The

first, third, seventh, thirteenth, twenty-fifth, and thirty-third are especially important. On anniversaries—weddings, birthdays, deaths—we recall the events quietly. The memorial service makes public our grief. It gives us permission to mourn.

Services are not only meant for memorials but also for congratulatory things. On these occasions the spirit is more a sense of gratitude. We Buddhists believe that all things are interdependent, that what I am and how I came to be was not done by my own power alone but with the support and the help of the karmic forces of all beings.

Buddhists touch this karmic force through deep meditation. Essentially what happens in deep meditation is that the mind is still so that there are no extraneous thoughts that enter into the mind, no uncontrolled thoughts that arise from the mind. When the mind is very still, what happens, the Buddhist documents say, is that there's a kind of focus, a kind of mindfulness. When mindfulness happens, there's a feeling of zest, a feeling of joy, a feeling of oneness with all things. Technically what happens is that when the mind is very still, it becomes like a great mirror. This mirror is able to reflect all things and all beings with fidelity and without any prejudice. The meditative state is not a condition that can be maintained for a period of time; one must descend from this high, rarified meditative state. But one emerges from this condition with this feeling of zest, of joy, of oneness. These feelings help. The world is a pretty hard place to make our way through.

After meditation we become less judgmental. The meditative state teaches us to look at people quietly and without prejudice. We are more accepting of people and their faults, and I think this helps in our relationships with other people.

I like to think meditation also affects my work. After meditation not only do I relate to people better, I'm able to work better. I'm more nonjudgmental. Meditation also teaches us to see people and their needs more clearly, so we're able to help people in a much more objective and beneficial way. I'm able to read people better, and if I'm able to read people better, I'm able to help them better.

Meditation leads to wisdom, wisdom leads to clarity and seeing justice. Wisdom is also very positive; we must use this wisdom to relieve the sufferings of others. This is what we call engaged Buddhism. In conjunction with that, there is also the idea that meditation is not a quiescent state but a very dynamic state. The act of compassion, whatever it may be, is itself an act of great meditation. For myself personally I take this to be the highest form of meditation. Here we have a focus of mind on being what will uplift humanity. That is the activity of wisdom and the implementation of wisdom. Wisdom and compassion—*upaya*. It is actually the highest form of enlightenment. Meditation in action. The stillness and the movement are one.

For Buddhists the important thing is to try. We know that ideals, becoming the Buddha, are difficult if not impossible to achieve. But these ideals are our vision of what humanity should be. There was a Vietnamese monk, Thieh Nhat Hanh, who said, "When I want to go to the North Star, it doesn't mean that I will ever get there. What is important is that I move in that direction." It is important that we move in the direction of compassion.

MARLENE PAYNE

*Marlene Payne, M.D., has been a psychiatrist in private prac-
tice in McLean, Virginia, for sixteen years and assistant clinical
professor of psychiatry at Georgetown University for fifteen
years. An active member of the Church of Jesus Christ of
Latter-day Saints, she has published articles in a variety of Mormon books and periodicals. She and her husband, John D.
Payne, have been married for twenty years. They have three
children.*

Prayer is a conversation between me and my Father in
Heaven. In terms of Mormon theology we think that we
existed as intelligences for a long time and then were
born as spirit children to a father and mother in Heaven.
God consists of male and female. We lived with them for
a long time and grew to a certain point, then they created this world for us to come to and have a physical
mother and father. The expectation is also that we will
work to return to their presence, that we will use the
light of Christ and knowledge of good and evil that we
have and the Gospel plan that we have in the church to
try to return to their presence. So when I pray, I pray to
my Father in Heaven, and He is a person and I am His
child.

I talk to him as I would to another person. I ask Him
to help me with things that are of concern in my life, in
my immediate family's life, in my extended family's life.
I ask His blessing upon the leaders of the nation and the

church, upon people that I know that are sick or having a hard time. I especially ask His help for my children, to watch over them and protect them and help guide them through all the trials and temptations of adolescence. I ask blessings for my husband and his health and strength and peace of mind. I ask blessings for my own spiritual needs, to have the strength to do His will, to be humble in my life, and to love other people. I ask for blessings sometimes for difficult situations such as Bosnia or Somalia.

I also try to give thanks. I know I really like to be thanked when I do something for people, so I think about the blessings of my life and express gratitude to Him for all the many blessings that He's ever given me. There's a really good feeling about that, because even at times when my life is hard and stressful, I also recognize how generally good He is to me and how good life is.

There are different levels of prayer that one enters into, and a lot of times it depends on the state of mind. There are times in life that are very, very hard. My husband's parents lived with us for two and a half years, and then they both died—my father-in-law after a year and a half, my mother-in-law after two and a half years. It was very demanding and draining. My mother-in-law was totally handicapped and sick and required total physical care. My father-in-law, though he wasn't as sick, wanted to go to a lot of doctors and needed a lot of stimulation and input, and so it, too, was very draining. I also had to deal with the rest of my family and my practice. I often prayed really fervently for strength during that time, and I remember one time when I was praying and I was really irritable and upset; I just couldn't get rid of that sense of irritability and the drains and demands that were placed upon me, and I asked the Lord to give me peace. It took about forty-five minutes, but then I felt this wonderful peace replacing the irritability and the anger, and it just stayed with me. That happened not just once but a number of times when I could just feel that gift being given. Because it was a good thing that I was doing, I felt that I was being taken care of and sustained.

The whole process of my praying has a foundation in the fact that I do try to live the Gospel as the Mormon religion has taught it to me. I try very hard to do things that keep me in tune with what my Heavenly Father would want me to be doing; that's the only way that I can feel comfortable asking for things when I pray. At times in my life—when I was in my late adolescence and early twenties—I was very rebellious, and it was very painful to pray because I felt guilty and ashamed, and hated to go to the Lord. It's much easier to pray when you're trying to live in tune with your principles. I feel like, "I've done my part, now please do your part."

In the Mormon church there's a sense that we follow the Gospels and do these good works, and the works are important because we do the Lord's work that way, and we grow through that. But there's also the concept of grace that the Protestants talk about. Grace, to my mind, is the part that I can't supply; it's the part that I ask the Lord for in prayer, the great filling up with the Holy Ghost, the inspiration, the guidance, the gift of knowing who needs help, the gift to be sensitive to other people's needs. I find that this gift is given; it will occur to me while I am praying: "Well, so-and-so needs something, they need help" and I'll call them or send a card or do something, and it turns out that they did need help. Both when I'm praying and when I'm reading the Scripture, these are times when the Holy Ghost will prompt me to think in terms of doing something compassionate for someone else.

I very much feel that God answers my prayers in terms

of the feelings that He gives to me, but I've also had direct answers to my prayers. Some people pray about all sorts of business things, such as "Should I sell my house for this much or this much, should I buy a new car right now, what kind of car should I get, gee, what year? How many repairs is it going to need?" I feel that the Heavenly Father doesn't need to be bothered with that stuff; that's really kind of petty. I know that some people feel that doing so means that they really rely on the Lord, but I tend not to ask for answers to questions like that.

I will ask for answers about—oh, I'm asked to give a lot of talks for my church and my community during the evening, when I'm really tired; I'm depleted mentally and physically. I will work on the talk, but on a few occasions where I would pray and ask for cognitive help, I would have answers given to me that were very clear—different from what I had laid out.

One experience was really very special to me. That was a time when I was praying and my thoughts were just bouncing off the ceiling. I wasn't connecting, I was feeling anxious and preoccupied by details of regular life, and I figured, "Well, I think I'll just stop praying this way and I'll just pray with my feelings." I guess what I used was visual imagery. I imagined my Father in Heaven sitting in a chair, in a magnificent chair, and I felt like my spirit went to Him and sat in His lap. I don't generally think that Heavenly Father has wings, but in this experience He did, and He put them around me, and they were very, very soft. They were so soft and warm, it was just wonderful. I felt a love from Him that was different from anything I've ever experienced on this earth. Our earth love, I think, is very limited and partial, but this love was so gracious and intense, and I felt like He just loved and accepted me for who I was. It wasn't that I had to be perfect, I was just loved. And I knew it wasn't just me, I knew this was how He loved all His children. I was experiencing part of the nature of God. It was the most wonderful feeling. It just removed my anxiety and made me feel my life was being lived in the right direction.

Sitting next to Him was Heavenly Mother, and she smiled this beautiful smile, and next to her was Christ, and I thought, "He is my brother." We Mormons believe that we are all the literal children of Father in Heaven, and as Christ was the first-born spirit, so he is my spiritual brother. After that experience my spirit came back into my body, but the Holy Ghost followed me and again put arms around me and comforted me.

This happened, I guess, about five or six years ago, but it has stayed with me and stayed with me and just been a source of real joy and comfort. At times when I have felt very alone and have suffered, I have remembered both this and my belief that I am a daughter of God, and they really help me. I never feel abandoned in life because of these experiences and because of the knowledge that I can connect with my Father in Heaven through prayer. It was really a transcendental experience for me.

Prayer in groups is a whole other aspect of prayer. I pray with my children in family prayer, and then they have their individual prayers at night, and we say a blessing on the food before our meals. In our family prayers people take turns saying them; we did this in my family growing up also. The father appoints someone to pray. As my husband is not Mormon, I am the one to pick in my own family now. The person who prays will say a prayer thanking Heavenly Father and asking blessings on the family. Sometimes the children will also use it to manipulate each other: "Bless J.D. that he won't bug me anymore." So we tell them, "Prayers are not weapons. This is the Creator of the universe; have respect."

I, too, have always prayed since I was tiny. I did individual prayers by my bed at night for as long as I can remember. When I was really little, those tended to be more rote prayers. And that's what my own children currently say: the same things over and over every night. But when they get to be about six or seven, I'll say, "You need to pray from your heart and talk to Heavenly Father about the things that worry you or make you happy, about what happened during the day and what's happening the next day." As they get older, it becomes more real for them, and I can remember that happening to me.

Each week my family goes to church on Sunday for three hours. We have a grand meeting all together, and then people split up for Scripture study, and then there's another meeting where women meet together, men meet together, and children meet together. We have many prayers throughout that time. The meeting where we take the sacrament begins with a prayer, and then there are two prayers on the bread and the water, and then we close with a prayer. And then there's an opening prayer to Sunday school and a closing prayer, an opening prayer to the women's meeting and a closing prayer. Those prayers are offered by all of us as a group, and people take turns praying before the group. It is not a set prayer but a prayer from the heart for the people in our church jurisdiction and the bishop who leads us, and then prayers for the whole church and the nation.

We have set prayers over the sacrament that are very beautiful and that remind us of the covenant that we made at the time of baptism: to remember Christ and to take his name upon us. They're beautiful because I've heard them every week of my life since I was born. The prayers are preceded by a song that's very serene and gets you in the mood. Then the prayers are given, and while the sacrament is being passed, we pray and meditate. As my children have gotten older, I actually have been able to do that; when they were younger, they would interrupt me all the time. I feel such a sense of renewal and peace from the experience.

The Mormon Sunday meetings are held in our chapel. Our chapels are local, and there are many, many around this area. But there's only one temple, and that temple covers a very large area all along the East Coast. I'm fortunate enough to be just twenty-five minutes from it. I go there once a month. There's a set ritual there, which I am not at liberty to discuss, but it does include prayer in which people hold hands, and it is very sacred and special. There is a sense of strength that flows into you.

In terms of my relationship with other people, prayer is very helpful because it enables me to see people in a more compassionate light and to forgive. I pray to have a much more peaceful and tolerant attitude toward my husband. I mean, I love him anyway—we have a very good marriage—and he's a wonderful man, so that's not real hard. But it helps keep the tone of the marriage much sweeter, and it helps me to let go of the little irritations that come up. With my children I pray for patience and for understanding. I know sometimes that when I'm tired, I lose my patience. I also spend a lot of time praying on behalf of my children for help with whatever they're going through.

In terms of my work, I pray about difficult patients. Sometimes patients will ask me to pray for them, and I do pray for them and for their well-being. I know that there are limits to what we people can accomplish, but the Lord doesn't have any limits.

In terms of the larger community, I do pray for peace in difficult areas of the world and for people who need the Lord's blessings, but I am not much of a political person. I don't go to community political meetings and I barely read the paper. I have opinions about politics, but I don't write letters, I don't get involved. I barely have the time and energy for my family and my practice, so the larger world is not much better for my presence in it, I guess, except that I'm keeping my own little part of it in pretty good order.

When my family is grown, if I have a time in my life that I have more choice in what I do, I'd like to work on behalf of the homeless. They really need psychiatric help because about half, I think, were dumped out of Saint Elizabeth's Hospital when D.C. closed it. About half are schizophrenic or manic-depressive, and they are untreated. I'd really like to work on their behalf. If I did that, then I would be able to pray about it in a much more personal way. I'd be able to pray on behalf of people I'd be working with and programs I was actually involved in. That's the kind of effect on the larger community that I would like to have. My life is lived in terms of these intimate relationships and personal involvements, the one-on-one work with patients. The things that I pray about, that are the most heartfelt, are my intimate relationships. And the older I get, the more heartfelt my prayers become.

JANE REDMONT

Jane Redmont is the author of Generous Lives: American
Catholic Women Today. *A graduate of Harvard Divinity
School, she has worked in ministerial positions as a Catholic lay-
woman in both campus and urban parish settings. At the time
of the interview she was the northeastern regional director for the
National Conference (founded as the National Conference of
Christians and Jews).*

I think of prayer primarily as listening. I also experience
it as conversation. I understand it as being in the presence of God with more attention than usual, because I
think one is *always* in the presence of God. I see God's
presence in a lot of different ways. The older I get, the
more Catholic I'm becoming, in that I have a very incarnational kind of theology; everything can reveal God:
people, nature, suffering, making love, even sadness and
death.

I'm a very eclectic pray-er. I don't have one way of
praying. Although I pray in a lot of different ways—some
quiet and some noisy, some solitary and some communal—I think I always return to the core, which is found
in the contemplative tradition.

I became a Catholic in my early twenties. I was raised
a Unitarian-Universalist, and my grandparents and most
of my ancestors were Jewish. One grandfather became a
Christian Scientist. My parents became Unitarians the
year they were married. I was a Calvinist Girl Scout in

France for seven years. The Scouts in France are denominational: they have Catholic Scouts, Protestant Scouts, Eastern Orthodox Scouts, Jewish Scouts, and neutral Scouts. My parents' closest French friends were members of the French Reformed church and had been part of that church's scouting movement, so that's why my brother and I got packed off to it.

Our Girl Scout camp was very outdoorsy, with dirt and hiking and building your own fire. We would get together on Sunday morning up there in the mountains, and somebody would pick a Bible reading, and somebody would pick a couple of hymns, and there'd be twelve of us sitting around in a circle on the grass doing this little worship service. I didn't think about it until years later, when I realized that this had been my first experience with a small, grassroots, lay-led prayer experience.

My conversion started in my teenage years, perhaps before. When I was a child, we were close to the Society of Friends because the Unitarian Fellowship my parents founded in Paris used to meet at the International Quaker Center, and my family would sometimes take part in the activities there, too. I used to accompany my mother to Friends Meeting. In college I went to Friends Meeting once in a while and almost never to the Unitarian worship services. I was also studying and practicing Buddhist meditation. Then I discovered there was a contemplative tradition in the West, too, and I started exploring that. I was drawn to the depth of it and the quiet. I remember Brother David Steindl-Rast, a Benedictine monk, coming to speak at Oberlin when I was a student there, and relating his experience of encountering some Eastern monks; although they were from completely different traditions, they had something in common that was so profound, they almost didn't need words for it. Something powerful happened to me that day, hearing that. All the contemplative traditions—whether they involve Centering Prayer (an ancient form of Christian contemplative prayer), or meditation, or another technique—are very similar in the inner stillness one touches.

I have a fairly stormy inner life much of the time, but that doesn't bother me because I know it's a part of the contemplative life. It's a part of having a relationship with God—or, if you don't want to talk about it in those terms, part of any experience of sitting in meditation. You're always going to run into your own inner turmoil. At this point in my life I just kind of say "Hi" to it when I encounter it, because I know it's par for the course in the spiritual life. Of course there are times when inside it feels like the desert, or like being lost, or as if I'm drowning, but for the most part there is a kind of peace in the chaos.

I do have a daily spiritual practice that is solitary and that helps me in the really demanding job I'm in right now. I get up in the morning and do a little bit of hatha yoga. Before I rush into the very busy urban life I have, I do something with my body to quiet my mind and my heart, because even before I get up, things are already racing. Then I meditate. Sometimes it's simply meditation and sometimes I practice Centering Prayer; I find there's a very fine line between the two. Then I make the sign of the cross and pray a little. Without words. Or with words. I used to read the Bible in the morning, but I don't much anymore. The whole thing probably takes a total of twenty minutes. I know you're supposed to do yoga for longer and you're supposed to meditate for at least twenty minutes. For a while I set that as a standard for myself, but when I didn't end up doing it, I felt guilty. So I decided it's better to be faithful to a little something every day than not to do it at all and fill my life with *shoulds* and *oughts*.

I talk to God throughout the day, or I listen. Often it's pretty primitive stuff: "Help" or "Give me strength." Sometimes something absolutely wonderful, even a little thing, will happen in the middle of the day, and I'll take thirty seconds to say thank you. I'm much more aware these days of the need to say thank you.

I talk to Jesus a lot more than I used to. When I first became a Christian, I didn't experience what all the cat-echists say happens—that it starts with a relationship with Jesus and then moves on to other dimensions of God. I had a very strong experience of God as Spirit, I had a very strong experience of church, and those things are what led me into the church. Having a relationship with the person Jesus is something that developed much, much later, and is one that still sort of comes and goes for me. It's very strong right now. I'm white but I've spent a fair amount of time in black churches, and I do have friends who are Evangelical, so I know people for whom it's very natural to say, "Thank you, Jesus." I think I've picked that up, which is unusual for a left-wing Catholic intellectual.

Communal prayer is very important to me. I go to Sunday Eucharist. That's a whole different experience from my morning routine, but it feels connected to it. I go to the Paulist Center in Boston, one of those nonterritorial Catholic communities. It's got all sorts of problems and tensions, but so does every other place, and I have a group of peers there with whom I pray. I'm very attached to them and I'm very attached to the fact that we pray together. I feel very deeply connected to this group of people because I know we have similar val-ues and a common faith, and we sit there week after week together on Sundays singing and praying and strug-gling. The repetition of it, the layering of Sunday upon Sunday, changes me and changes them. I wish there were more quiet spaces in that particular liturgy, but I do love the singing and the kids crawling all over the pews and the community and the Eucharist.

About ten or twelve years ago I hit a time when I couldn't pray. I just couldn't. I was pretty depressed that year. I haven't had a time like that since. I was bereft emotionally and spiritually. Well, as I look back, it was one of the most significant times in my prayer life, because I was truly carried by the prayer of others, by the prayer of the community. I was in another parish, Saint Ann's, and I would go there Sundays, and I learned that you don't have to do it all yourself, that you can pray even when you yourself can't pray, when you have no words, when you have no strength. You just put yourself inside the prayer of the church, and it cradles you. It moves you along. It holds you up.

A lot of my communal prayer life has been as a leader of prayer. As a Catholic laywoman in ministry I've had as much of a liturgical leadership role as one can have in a public celebration, including reading the Gospel, preaching at Sunday Eucharist, and copresiding at baptisms and weddings. I also officiate at weddings alone because I'm a justice of the peace here in Massachusetts. Sometimes it's easier for me to pray, or at least I feel more of a sense of guidance, when I'm having to do it for others. I listen and hear God's voice a lot when I'm writing homilies. I'll pore over the Scriptures and read commentaries and analyze and study for hours and pray, and then I'll write the thing and I have no idea where the words came from. I know that some of it is not from me.

I'm in a group right now with folks from the Paulist Center, women and men who work in various managerial positions in downtown Boston: lawyers, bankers, a physician, a nonprofit executive. We call it the Faith and Work Group, and it's not really a prayer group. We do pray at the beginning and at the end, but mostly we reflect together on what our faith and our work have to do with each other. I don't really expect answers or solutions to all the dilemmas we face, but it's nice to have company ... and to speak the same language, to bring God into the picture.

When I was social justice minister at the Paulist Center, the various social justice groups I worked with always had four components—I insisted upon it. They were action, prayer, study or reflection, and celebration. If you don't have those four things, you run into problems. They're all necessary to bringing about social justice. You have to know where you're rooted. I also think that celebration, fiesta, partying is very important. You shouldn't be running around with a long face all the time; it's not going to make the world any better.

I've always mostly made up prayers as I go. But two very interesting things have happened, and they both have to do with Mary. I've been very surprised at that because when I became a Catholic, Mary and the saints were the last folks I thought I'd hook up with. But really I've become quite attached to them. In the research for my book I heard all these Catholic women talk about the saints, and now I agree with them that there is a lot of company out there in the journey of faith; it's very comforting.

My third year in divinity school was the first year I was a Catholic, and it was a spiritually barren year for me. The year before had been full of a sense of the presence of God and all sorts of consolation, and as soon as I got baptized and received into the church, bingo! The big desert. I had a horrendous year. There were no spiritual goodies to be found. It was a very trying time in my inner life. I was in the process of breaking up with, or being broken up with by, the man I thought I was going to marry. It was winter, it was cold, it was just miserable. I

found myself saying Hail Marys that winter, just Hail
Marys, not the Rosary, when walking home from school
in the cold. Prayer became sort of an anchor in the
storm.

The other time Mary made an impact was more recent, but it had its genesis about ten years ago. The pastor of the church I was attending at the time took me
aside one day at a party and said, "You know, if you're
ever really having a rough time, you should pray the
Memorare." The prayer is, "Remember, O most gracious
Virgin Mary, that never was it known that anyone who
fled to thy protection, implored thy help, and sought thy
intercession was left unaided. Inspired with this confidence, I fly unto thee, O Virgin of Virgins, my Mother.
To thee I come, before thee I stand sinful and sorrowful.
O Mother of the Word Incarnate, despise not my petitions but in thy mercy hear and answer me. Amen." He
then went back to drinking Scotch, or whatever it was
he was doing.

Now, I wasn't raised with Catholic devotions. Nor did
I go seeking them. I've been much more the type to sit
cross-legged and meditate, and I still do that. But I
prayed the *Memorare* two summers ago, when I was finishing my book. I thought the project would never be
done; I'd been working on this damned book on Catholic women for five years, I had no money left, I was
deeply in debt, my family thought I was nuts because I
was still working on it and not earning a decent living,
I was way past my deadline, and I would sit at the computer crying and tapping out the words. I taught myself
the *Memorare* that summer. I memorized it; I didn't know
it before. And I said it all summer and all fall until I finished the book. I prayed that prayer, and again it was a
kind of an anchor in the storm. It really was a prayer of
desperation, absolute, utter, total desperation.

So that's my experience with set prayers: they tend to be Mary prayers. I do say the Lord's Prayer quite a bit also. I'm not particularly comfortable with God as Father, so I kind of stumble over the first words, but that prayer has been important to me for a long, long time. I try to say it very slowly.

I'm also extraordinarily fond of one of the traditional Jewish blessings. It's the one that says, in the traditional version, "Blessed art thou O Lord our God, king of the universe, who has kept us in life and sustained us and enabled us to reach this season." You say it when you've reached a particularly wonderful day in your life, or, as one of my friends says, when you've eaten the first peach of the season or your child takes her first steps or when you're just glad to be alive. Rather than the old translation, I now prefer one used by synagogues that pray with inclusive language. It goes like this: "Holy One of Blessing, your presence fills creation. You have kept us alive, you have sustained us, you have brought us to this moment."

When I realized that I was going to be in this very highfalutin, close-to-the-corporate-world job, I decided I was going to memorize the Beatitudes and recite them on the subway on the way to work. I've now stopped, but the first month or two there I was in my pearls and high heels mumbling, "Blessed are the poor in spirit." I did it so that I would keep my priorities straight.

The rest of the time my prayer is rambling and doesn't have words. I'm also a great, great music lover, and music has been a major part of my spiritual life. I think that I was partially converted by Mozart. My first year in college was the year that the Kent State killings happened; my whole college closed down and went to Washington. At this stage I was very concerned about the Vietnam War, but I wasn't very political. I didn't know how to lobby. I was a U.S. citizen but had just moved here from Europe the year before. I wasn't very comfortable doing straightforward political action, but I wanted to protest the war.

It turns out that the choir at Oberlin College decided to throw together Mozart's Requiem in three days. For this you didn't have to audition; anybody could do it. They suspended the rules. So I was part of this wonderful chorus that sang Mozart's Requiem after the big rally in Washington in May 1970 in the National Cathedral. At the time I was still officially a Unitarian. It was one of the most powerful religious experiences I've ever had. It truly was an experience of prayer, with singing and being in the middle of that music. And those are words I come back to a lot, words that I learned not by going to Mass and not by memorizing them, but by singing Mozart. They come back to me at times when very dear friends die.

I love jazz and Gospel; I like folk Masses and plainsong. I spent time at the Taizé community the year after I finished college—that's the ecumenical monastery in Burgundy whose music is wonderful, it has a very singable chant, which I still listen to on tape and sing by myself at home. Bach was very important to me as a teenager, and I came back to him when I was writing my book. I used to play guitar and sing, and I've had classical voice lessons, so I could sing *Lieder* and arias. For me all of this is prayer.

Sometimes it's hard for me to differentiate the times of prayer and the times of nonprayer, because I feel that I'm always in the midst of prayer. I don't feel that I'm ever outside that kind of moment. I sometimes pray for guidance, yes. How do I know if I get it? It's when I have a sense of clarity and very deep peace, and feel connected to myself and the world in a way that makes sense. In terms of vocational questions there needs to be not just a sense of inner call and peace but some sense of outer call, a sense that other people are calling me to do something. That's been true with the ministry jobs I've been in, and with my sense of ministerial and priestly vocation.

One of the most powerful experiences of prayer I've had is the AIDS Healing Service in Boston. It's sponsored by the Ecumenical Task Force on AIDS here; it's a sort of a traveling road show. Every couple of weeks a different church hosts a healing service for anyone concerned about AIDS. It can be people with AIDS, it can be their caregivers or their friends, or people who are just worried and wish it would go away. It's usually done in the style of the denomination that happens to be hosting it. My church hosted one of these services the other night, and I was one of the "ministers of healing." That meant that we did laying on of hands and prayed with whomever came up to us with a request for prayer. There was some singing, and there were prayers and Scripture readings and a homily, and then there was music, and teams of two or three ministers of healing went off to the four corners of the chapel. People came up to us alone, or sometimes in pairs, and asked for whatever they wanted prayed for, and then we would lay hands on them or embrace them or offer whatever the appropriate physical touch seemed to be. I was allegedly the minister of healing, but *I* felt very healed by the whole experience.

I think some of that had to do with this very ancient gesture of laying on of hands. People need to be touched. There's a real spiritual power in that touching. Also people were just honest about who they were. There were all kinds of folks there; they were from different social and educational backgrounds, and some were straight and some were gay. When people were coming up to be prayed with, they said all sorts of things about what was going on in their lives. No one wore any masks. A lot of the things that were shared were very sad, but it wasn't a brutal honesty; there was a gentleness in it. The person who was assigned to be my partner in this ministry of healing turned out to be a man I hadn't seen in ten years, whom I knew from divinity school. What a way to meet again: holding people and finding words of prayer for them. The only good thing about the AIDS epidemic is that as much as it's brought forth all sorts of fear and hatred from people, it's also taught people how to love in a new way.

MARY FRANCES ROBLES

Mary Frances Robles is a single, working mother from Tucson, Arizona, who works in a print shop. She is a member of Our Mother of Sorrows Catholic Church in Tucson, where her daughter attends the parish school.

Prayer is a way of communicating your needs and your wants to God. It's a way of opening up to Him so that you can ask for forgiveness and guidance. It's a means of communicating.

I pray to God as Jesus, to Mother Mary and the Apostles, and to Saint Jude. Mostly I pray to God, but when I say, "Hail Mary, full of grace . . . ," I feel I'm praying to Mary. I pray to Saint Jude when I'm feeling down because he stands for those who are hurting or in need. It was my mom who taught me to pray to Saint Jude.

During the day I pray to God to guide me to do the right thing. It's usually for just a few minutes and happens at any time throughout the day. If something's not going right, I'll ask Him why. I'll ask Him to help me get through the moment. I'll ask, "Why is this happening?" If I'm by myself, I'll do it out loud. If there are people around, I'll say it to myself.

I often go to a Rosary service. Families and friends gather together at a designated house that someone has volunteered. We bring with us a picture of Our Lady of Guadalupe. Many people believe that Our Lady—the Virgin Mary—appeared to Juan Diego, a poor peasant at

Guadalupe, Mexico. We then say the "Our Father" and the "Hail Mary," and someone talks about something that's touched them in their lives—maybe someone had cancer and was healed. Then others open up and tell of their hopes or something that happened to them. We sing, usually in Spanish and in English. It's a way for us to get together and pray.

Prayer makes me feel at ease, for I know that God is listening. There's no sign right off the bat that He hears me, but I know He's listening and that makes me feel comfortable. Sometimes I overlook the fact that He's answered my prayers. I used to live at an apartment—it was just my daughter and myself—and I wasn't happy living there. I would ask Him please for something else. I would get frustrated and think, "There must be another way." A few weeks later a lady asked us to move in with her. So that's just one example of how He answered my prayers.

Prayer first became important to me as a child. My mom was the one who taught us how to pray. She told us not to ask for material things, for they weren't important. When I was going through problems, prayer helped me. Sometimes I used to just recite the prayers, the Rosary, or the Our Father without thinking about what the words meant. Now I realize the prayers are more than just words. When I would say, "Our Father who art in Heaven, Hallowed be Thy name," I would do so only because I knew them by heart. But now I see that it's talking about God in Heaven and how He wants us to look to Him. I used to have the same attitude about Mass; I used to go to church every Sunday just as a routine. Now I realize that when I don't go, I'm missing something. One day and one hour out of the week is the *least* I can do. Plus, I feel that as an example for my daughter I should attend Mass.

My mother also taught me that when I needed to talk

to someone, I should pray to God. She said that when we were feeling down, He was the one to turn to. My daughter is sometimes afraid to go to bed at night; she's only seven, and she's afraid of things. I told her to talk to God and to tell Him anything she feels. I told her that He's always with us. That's what I want her to know. So she shares her feelings and her thoughts with Him. Now we pray together almost every night, and she feels better afterward. It's a way of releasing her feelings; she's not afraid at night after she prays. She likes us to pray together. Some nights, if it's real late, she'll have to pray by herself, but even then she makes sure she does pray. I don't have to force her, she just does. We say the Our Father and the Hail Mary, and then anything else that we want to say—thanking God for the day and for things that happened, asking Him to help us to get along a little better in the morning and not be rushed when we're getting up. To us God is real and God is here. It's a good feeling to have talked to Him.

EVE RUDIN

Eve Rudin works for the Department of Youth Activities of the Union of American Hebrew Congregations, the Reform Jewish movement. She graduated from Brandeis University with a B.A. in Judaic Studies. She also plays the violin.

There are two types of prayer for Jews. One is structured prayer—not necessarily communal, but structured—that is part of the liturgy; it praises God, gives thanks, and also asks for things. Some of these prayers cover cycle events. Structured prayer is known as *keva*. The other type of prayer is *kavanah*; it's what *you* bring to prayer, or it's any personal time where you are in thought.

I consider prayer to be anytime that I'm deep in thought about anything. I also think about prayer as anytime I communicate with God or anytime that I'm keyed in to a cycle event—a life or a holiday cycle. For me cycles, such as the Jewish holiday cycle or the life cycle, which comprises weddings, deaths, births, are very important; and anytime my life is going from one stage to another, where it is showing some kind of growth, is a cycle event.

But I would also say that anytime that I wish someone to drive safely, I consider myself praying. I probably pray a little everytime I get into a car—especially in bad weather. Some of the time I pray before I eat. When I'm at home with my parents, we always pray before we eat. And when I'm in my camp setting—I work with Jewish youth, and we try to provide a religious atmosphere—we say a prayer before and after meals. During a regular day I'd probably say that I pray about 50 percent of the time, regardless of where I am.

Prayer also occurs during the day when you wake up, and when you feel tired and want the day to end—anything like that. There are Jewish prayers for all sorts of daily cycle events, such as waking up, going to the bathroom, getting dressed, and so on. Although I don't say those prayers formally, I consider the fact that I don't take those things for granted a form of prayer.

On a typical day the only liturgy or set-out prayers that I say would be before I go to sleep, when I say Sh'ma, which is the basic prayer that says that God is one. Many Jews say it before they go to sleep: "Hear, O Israel, the Eternal is our God, God is one."

When I was in high school, I was very involved in the North American Federation of Temple Youth (NFTY), which is the organization that I work for now. It's Reform Judaism's youth movement. The type of prayer found in these settings is a mixture of some Hebrew prayers and some English poetry or creative reading. NFTY is geared toward high school kids, who often feel uncomfortable going out to regular synagogues with the more structured "adult" type of prayer. NFTY will have the basic Hebrew prayers and then poems and creative readings about a theme—freedom, or friendship, or shabbat, or anything. I've since grown out of that type of prayer—although I still see its importance for the high school students with whom I work. I used to pray that way, but during my college career I learned more Hebrew and became comfortable praying in an Orthodox atmosphere where it was all Hebrew. I was drawn to the traditional Jewish prayers because I like the feeling that the words I'm saying out of the prayer book are words that

Jews all around the world are saying. There is time for personal prayer in the liturgy, but I've become very connected to the idea of the tradition that goes on, and that is that all Jews on Friday evenings are saying the same thing, with their own personal additions.

I don't pray in small groups unless you count when something terrible happens and there's a group reaction. Something tragic happened to someone in our office a few weeks ago, and when we found out about it, we were all saying "How awful!" and "This is terrible." It was in a way a small group prayer.

I have never been one to ask for material things. When I have my moment for silent prayer, I usually ask for peace and understanding between other human beings. I ask for strength, I ask for the ability to be logical and rational in a decision I'm making. I've never asked for money or an item. As to the answers I've received, I saw an answer of sorts when my grandfather died. He was eighty-seven, and I didn't find it to be a horribly sad and traumatic experience because I was able to recognize that this man had lived everything he had ever wanted. He was very interested in education and family and he had done everything that he had set out to do. So I saw his death as a celebration of his life, for God had let him accomplish so much. For me the fact that some people do get to do what they want to do was sort of a prayer being answered. It wasn't an answer to a specific prayer, but I felt God's presence in that there was some justice in my grandfather's life and death. He had had the opportunity to live a full life.

Generally I feel more at peace with myself after prayer, and this helps me be more productive. Prayer reminds me of who I am and helps me set my priorities, and in the case of Shabbat, the priorities for the upcoming week. Shabbat is a time when you're supposed to rest and look back on the week and think about what's coming up. After praying I definitely feel that I've taken a step back and rested, and then I feel ready to attend to my priorities for the next week. I also feel that I'm part of something bigger.

Most of my friends are Jews, and religious Jews at that. I believe that God gave everyone free will, and you choose to pray. I've chosen to pray and I feel like it's my choice. I don't think that God rules over the world and makes miraculous decisions, just as God does not rule over my life; I make my own decisions.

I would say that probably because I am involved in Judaism, and not just in prayer, I'm a good listener. One of Judaism's things is to welcome the stranger and to help people. In terms of my friendships it does affect me in that I am often a very giving person, a good listener. I try to be patient with people, and I accept the fact that if someone isn't like me, that's fine; everyone is an individual. Judaism stresses individuality, that not everyone is the same. I appreciate diversity, and it's probably because of my religion. We have free will, so prayer may guide me to make choices in one way, but it may guide someone else to make choices in another way.

I also find that I don't relate that well to people who aren't involved in religion. I've had some friends who actually pray all the time—they grew up Orthodox—but they don't really pray, they don't know what it means. They do the whole Jewish thing out of guilt, and not from the heart, and that is a big barrier for me.

I've always gotten along with, but never really been close to, non-Jewish people. I grew up in New York City and went to high school with many non-Jewish people, but I've never been in a social scene where I constantly meet them and befriend them. I have friends who went to the Jewish school Yeshiva when they were younger who are now very uncomfortable around non-Jewish people. I am not. I sometimes feel that there's a difference between us, and there is, and I am sure that they feel that way toward me, but I've never had any animosity toward non-Jews, unless they're anti-Semitic.

I don't meditate, but there is a service done at many of the youth events called a *Havdallah* service—it separates Shabbat from the rest of the week—which is very mystical. One thing it uses is a *niggon*, a wordless tune that originates in Hasidic Judaism. There are no words to it, it's just a tune—a la-la-la type of thing. People get very carried away by it, and that's very meditative.

But communal prayer doesn't always happen all the time for everyone; not everyone's in the mood. I've gone to synagogue and not been in the mood to pray, and it was almost meaningless. So personal prayer can be much more important, and Judaism recognizes this. There's more meaning in the personal prayers that come up during the day. Seeing a beautiful mountain or something is a prayer. Cycle events, nature, any recognition that something is beautiful, is a prayer. That's one reason why I like Jewish prayer—it reflects an understanding of people and it just makes a lot of sense.

ROBERT SCHULLER

Robert Schuller, a minister in the Reformed Church in America, is pastor of the Crystal Cathedral in Orange County, California, and host of the television program "The Hour of Power."

I define prayer as the human practice of connecting with the transcendent eternal spirit that we call God. I'm a Christian, so that's my frame of reference, and in the Bible we're taught to pray constantly.

I think prayer has different levels. The first level of prayer is positive thinking. If I think positively, my mind is open and receptive, positive about what can come. When I'm opening my mind to welcome unexpected moods, impulses, and ideas, that's the first level of prayer.

The second level of prayer would normally be called petition; it's where I directly appeal to God for something that I need or want. That's okay to do, because God wants me to develop myself and be the best person I can.

The third level of prayer would be intercession, where I'm not even asking for me, but for you and others.

The level higher than that would be praying where I'm practicing thanksgiving and praising God. My daughter lost her leg in a terrible motorcycle accident. When I heard, the prayer that I said was a thank-you: "Thank you, God, that she's alive. Thank you, God, that she just lost one leg. Thank you, God, that her face wasn't smashed. Thank you that her brain wasn't injured.

Thank you that they got her to the hospital." At those times that's the only way to pray.

Then there's a level above that that I call two-way prayer, where I don't praise God, don't thank Him, and don't even petition or intercede for others; it's where I just ask questions and wait for answers. I feel and receive guidance. That is almost the highest level of prayer because it's turning me into the person that God wants—not to get what I want, but to become the person that I *ought* to be.

The level of prayer above that—the highest level—would be the actions I take that bless people. I pay attention, I care about them, I listen to them, I feel for them. And in the process of being that kind of a caring human being I am praying at the highest level. Prayer at the highest level is glorifying God, and I glorify God when I become a really generous and caring person.

I know I've gotten an answer to prayer when I feel it and I know it. It's intuition probably. I was a friend of Karl Menninger and Victor Frankl, and both of them said, "Schuller, you're the most intuitive guy I've ever met." When I asked them, "What is intuition?" they both said, "I don't know." I personally think intuition is a powerful channel of the human psyche where God is allowed, through His holy spirit, to penetrate our consciousness. That's what I mean by, "I know that I know that I know that I know."

I run every morning, and that's prayer time for me. I always pray with my wife before we have our food, and always we pray together at bedtime. And then during the course of the day, when I'm looking at or listening to people, it's not at all uncommon for me to just sit quietly and open the sunroof on the top of my head and feel the light coming down; the prayer that I will say is that God should guide my mind so that I hear what I should hear, react the way I should react, and not just sit there as an inactive or a reactive person. I want to become a genuinely *proactive* person, so that I know what decision I should make here and now.

I don't use set prayers very often. I've written loads of them, but I don't use them much. I have favorite prayers, of course, that I love, like the Lord's Prayer, Francis of Assisi's famous prayer, and the Serenity Prayer of Niebuhr: "God, grant me the serenity to accept the things I cannot change, courage to change the things I can, and wisdom to know the difference." My religious roots are in the Dutch Reformed church, and unlike the Episcopal church or the Roman Catholic church, we don't have the same memorized ritual prayers.

If you were to ask me why I believe in prayer and how I know it's not superstition, my answer would be that I have profound admiration, respect, and love for a religious leader named Jesus Christ. He practiced prayer, He believed in it, He taught it, and I think He knew what He was doing. And I'm with Him.

DAN SEALS

Dan Seals is a singer and songwriter who lives in Henderson-
ville, Tennessee. His career has spanned both rock and country
music. His hits include "Bop," "Good Timin'," "You Still Move
Me," "If I Had Only One Friend Left," and "Rage On." He
is a member of the Baha'i faith, which has more than five million
members worldwide. Baha'is believe that Bahaullah, a Persian
nobleman (1817–1892) from Tehran, was a Divine Messenger
in the tradition of Abraham, Krishna, Moses, Zoroaster, Bud-
dha, Christ, and Muhammad.

I was raised a Southern Baptist, and we prayed, but when
I became a Baha'i, obligatory prayer was very new to me.
Before, we were pretty loose with our prayers; we prayed
a lot in church but then didn't pray so much during the
week unless we really wanted something or it was to heal
somebody. To say hello and check in and all of that as
something that you *have* to do was new for me. But after
I started doing it, it was a comfort, because it was something that I had to remember to do.

The Baha'i prayer book has specific prayers that
Bahaullah left for specific situations. Until that time I'd
only known one prayer that was left like that; Jesus left
the Lord's Prayer as a guide to go by. Suddenly here was
a wealth of prayers in a language that was different. They
ended with praising God with specifics such as "Thou art
the unknowable, the all-powerful, the all-wise. Saying
those things made me feel good, for I was praising the

deity that made us all. They all start, "O my God . . . ,"
but they don't have the word *Amen* at the end of them
because that's a word that means "so be it," or "that it
will be fulfilled." As Baha'is we believe that it has been
fulfilled, so there is no ending except to praise the attributes of God.

I use those prayers in my daily life. I use the obligatory
prayers and I pray for specifics, whether it's the healing
of a family member or someone else that I know that's
sick. For these people I say the healing prayer that
Bahaullah wrote. There are also prayers for the dead, for
marriage, and for all kinds of truly specific things. It's
been a real enrichment to my life to have the words that
Bahaullah left, for they deal with these things and say it
a lot better than I do. The Manifestation of God's words
are more powerful than ours; anyone that's ever read the
Lord's Prayer realizes the potency and beauty of those
words as opposed to what we could make up on our own.
So I also use the Baha'i prayer book to pray for specifics
in my own life: to gain qualities, to try to be a better father, and so on.

If I were to figure it out daily, I probably pray two or
three times a day. I pray the obligatory prayer at noon or
before sunset and then I pray in my own words a couple
of times a day. We open the Baha'i feast, which is every
nineteen days, with about four or five prayers.

There's also something very unique in this faith that
I've never seen before. There are five steps to prayer in
the Baha'i faith. It brings what people would usually
consider metaphysical things down to specifics. The first
step is to pray. The second step is to be very quiet and
still, and if you are, usually a flash of an answer comes at
that time. The third step is to find the determination to
do whatever that flash says to do. The fourth thing is to
go and do it tirelessly, with whatever power that you

have in order to accomplish it. The fifth step is to act as if your prayer has already been answered, to accept the fact that God has already answered it. Well, many times I've had a problem, and after quiet reflection at the end of the prayer a flash does come. Sometimes it's made no sense personally, so it was nothing I would just pull out of the air. When I went ahead and acted on it, it always solved the situation. So I believe very strongly in those five steps to prayer.

The way I feel after prayer depends upon the situation. If I pray for another individual who's very sick, I sometimes still carry the agitation of worry within me afterward. If I pray about something and put it in God's hands, I often just let go of it. Sometimes I can't—I'll be honest about that—and it still weighs on my mind. Although after prayer I feel calmer a lot of the time, sometimes I don't. Sometimes I feel like I don't connect, like I've missed the boat. I don't feel that God has left me or anything like that, I just feel that maybe I'm in the way, or that something I've done or said got in the way. I think the fear of God that we talk about is not the fear that God will strike us dead, hurt us, or roast us forever in burning hell; it's that something we've done will not allow us to make that connection with Him or to make it as easily as we have before. Prayer is like anything else: the more you do it, the better you get at it—at connecting, at putting things out of your mind. Sometimes I'm able to do it and sometimes, for whatever reason it may be, insecurity or something else, I feel like I'm kept back. Maybe I haven't connected because of myself. It's hard to get rid of self; it's with us all the time. Self, ego, the lower nature in man, gets in the way.

Music is my work and isn't usually part of my prayer. But I did ask people to pray in the shrines in Israel so that I could write a song that would bring people together in unity. I'd not been writing for a long time then, but a song immediately came to me. It's called, "We Are One," and it dealt with children in other countries. I often pray for the power to write songs, to continue with those thoughts wherever they come from. Sometimes I'll just be driving along in the car and get a great song idea. But if I go eight months without writing any songs that touch anybody, I pray that the creative flow will come through me, that I will get ideas for songs that will change the world and help my career. I do this mostly for selfish reasons: I'm in the business of music. This is the only job I have and the only job I've had for thirty years, so I've got to be successful in it because it's all I know how to do.

If there's something about somebody I don't like, I pray to forget their one bad quality and remember their nine good ones, or forget their nine bad qualities and remember the one good one. If there's been specifics prayed about, prayer sets the stage for my behavior to be different and to be open for a solution dealing with other people. Say you've got a kid that's doing something not so good, and you're trying to raise him and make him mature. You say prayers for the child to awaken and take more responsibility for his life, especially if he's a teenager. After you've said those prayers, it's out of your hands, and when you suddenly find he does grasp responsibility for himself, you feel like that's been an answer.

Obviously we're talking to an entity no one has even seen or smelt or tasted—although sometimes when I pray, I get the shivers physically: the hair on my arms stands up, or something like that. And then sometimes my heart feels like it's getting bigger in my chest; it's swelling or it's dilated. But that's the only physical feeling I have toward this deity that has created me, with the exception of one religious experience I had in the

Holy Land. I came face-to-face with something there that was unknowable and forceful and frightening and loving—everything all at one time. I can't say it was a real pleasant experience; it's not something that I would like to switch on at three o'clock every day. It was a one-time deal when I came in the presence of that Unknowable Essence. I don't claim to know God, and I don't think anybody on this earth can say, "Yeah, I know God, and I get through all the time." I think that this great power that made us all is unknowable and can't be sensed from the outer senses. But when I react physically to prayer, that lets me know that there's something there, as does having many, many prayers answered specifically, time after time after time. If I need something or want something and get it, I realize that only something on the other side of the wall there could be doing this.

I'm not a great person to ask about prayer. I'm more or less of a mule: I go around and I do the work and I plow the fields, but I don't know so much *why* I do it. I don't claim to tell anyone that I know anything, and I don't think anyone else does either. I love that movie where God was talking to John Denver and God told that evangelist he wanted him to sell shoes. People are getting answers, but I don't think the answers are the way they want them to be. If two thousand years ago Jews were in the synagogue praying for the Messiah to come and He was outside walking around in street clothes talking to whores in the street, they would have their prayers answered, but it would not have been in the way they wanted. Our answers to prayer can sometimes be a lot different from what everybody thinks. You and I could sit here and have a prayer saying, "I hope all Muslims and Christians will stop killing each other and be friends on this earth." Well, that will not happen as long as there are Muslims and Christians following the dogma and rituals that they uphold. In order for the Muslim and the Christian to love each other, they would have to walk away from their holy books and go out in a field somewhere and have something else touch them, to cause their hearts to love each other. Because if they keep following their own interpretations of the books in the way they've been doing, they'll just continue to kill each other. So if they're praying for peace, it won't happen in the way that they want.

Many years ago my grandfather was dying of cancer, and in my innocence I was down on my knees praying to Jesus to save him and bring him back and cure the cancer so that he could be with me longer. Well, that's a sixteen-year-old's attachment and innocence and wanting the hurt to stop. But my grandfather's time was up here; he was needed and being asked to go somewhere else. So I didn't get my prayer answered, and my grandfather died. What I really needed to be praying for was detachment from him and all things of this world, that the door between me and the Creator be kept open in some way, and that my grandfather be allowed to live his life and go on to the next world. The next world *has* to be the majority of our lives; this world is just a small portion of it. I didn't believe that back then, but in hindsight I realize that it was kind of silly for me to ask that my grandfather, who was in his eighties and completely eaten up with cancer, be saved; for what? He *was* healed all right; they said when he died, he was smiling, looking up at the ceiling and smiling. It sounds like he was going to a wonderful place if it made Granddad smile. He liked what was fixin' to happen to him, and immediately after that he ascended. He was healed, although it wasn't in the way I thought it would be.

As I aged, I grew to be detached from Granddad's physical presence, but I counted on his spiritual pres-

ence. I sometimes feel that he's near me or with me.
Sometimes I'll get a whiff of something in my nose that
reminds me of him, makes me feel he's around somewhere. I think the next world is pretty close to us, although I don't have a lot of weird things happen to me
the way some people do. I sometimes wish I did. I sometimes wish something would jump out of the clouds and
talk to me. I guess I need more faith or something, so
that I can stop looking for an outward, physical presence
from that world.

I love that movie *Resurrection* with Ellen Burstyn. Her
character is not religious; she just goes about and tries to
live her life innocently, tries to do the best she can. She
prays, she helps people, and she doesn't really have any
malice toward anyone. Then a kid gets hurt and she
holds the wound and suddenly he's healed. People come
to realize that she's the real thing—although her boy-
friend thinks that she's from the devil because she won't
go to church and subscribe to that life. People come to
her to be healed all the time, and this drives her crazy.
Finally she ends up out in the middle of nowhere in a
gas station. The last scene is when a little boy comes in.
He's got cancer and she wants to give him a dog. His
parents say he won't live very long to see this puppy. She
just goes over and gives him a real long hug, and the au-
dience knows what's happened, that he has been completely cured. She's obviously chosen now to help
people, one at a time without them knowing it. She
doesn't even want any money or notoriety for her healing power; she does it instead on her own terms. It was
a brilliant movie, and it changed me inside. I think we
all love those things because we all think about the next
world and hope it will be a wonderful, wonderful place.

ELEANA SILK

Eleana Silk is a graduate of and the librarian at Saint Vladimir's Orthodox Theological Seminary in Crestwood, New York. She is a member of the Orthodox Church in America's History and Archives Commission and is secretary of the Orthodox Christian Education Committee. She is the co-editor of The Legacy of St. Vladimir *(1990). Silk is also a computer programmer and systems analyst.*

Defining prayer is easy for me. Prayer is talking to God, during which you take almost the point of view of a child.

When I pray, I pray both silently and out loud—more silently than out loud. That might have to do with the fact that I'm a single person and live alone. If I were in a familial environment where there were more people around, there would be more communal prayer. As it stands now, I'm involved in communal prayer only at Saint Vladimir's. We have Matins every morning at seven-thirty and Vespers every night at five-thirty. We have this daily routine of services, and then we have feast-day services and Sunday liturgies. There's a complete liturgical cycle for the community.

In addition to that there's personal prayer. I don't get up in the morning and say my prayer in an orderly fashion, but there's a certain sense in which the whole day is offered up in prayer, and there are just periods of time when it comes out as a prayer. The prayer just bubbles up out of me. I can be walking home at lunchtime and it's a beautiful day outside, and I'll say, "Lord, thank you so much for this beautiful day and the fact that I'm able to appreciate it." It just comes bubbling up to the surface. Sometimes I'll say it out loud, as I'm walking, and people sometimes will look at me strangely.

But sometimes I feel that I don't need to have words in between God and myself; it's knowing that God is and I am, and that we are together. That's enough, and words aren't needed. Other times they are very much needed. An element of prayer develops because you memorize all the prayers. For example, I'm able to recite prayers like the Lord's Prayer and the Hail Mary. If there's a time in my life when I need prayer, a specific prayer just comes out. When you go through the liturgical cycle in the Eastern Orthodox church, it's rich in terms of poetry in the prayer, in terms of the music associated with the prayer. So sometimes my prayer is in music. When I'm praying, I'm singing; it's not just saying words or something that comes from rote. There's a melody of music that brings joy to the prayer as well.

We just went through Holy Week in preparation for Pascha a month ago, and it was really brought to my attention that I know a lot of the words to the Holy Week services. We're talking about services that are two and three hours long and that have been internalized in me as prayer. I don't know how it happened, but it did. I always wondered about that when I was a child: older people did the reading in church, and many times they read without a book; they didn't need to look at the words. I couldn't understand how they could learn all of that. It was beyond me. But now as I'm getting older, I feel that all of these words are inside of me, and they do come out at the right time.

Growing up in the church wasn't easy, because most of

the prayers were in Church Slavonic, and I didn't understand the language. But there was a message there that was above the words, and it somehow got communicated to me very early in my life. I couldn't explain the relationship that somehow developed between God and myself, but I knew that He was there, that He loved me, that I loved Him, and that I wanted that relationship not only now but eternally. This was an awareness on my part that I had when I was about eight or nine years old, and I recognized that I couldn't break the connection even if I wanted to, because God would always love me no matter what I did.

As a child I remember learning that there are prayers of asking or intercession, prayers of thanksgiving, and prayers of glorification. I think that the prayer of intercession is the one that children use most. Children think, "God, give me this, I want this thing" or "Help me to do this." The "me" is much more the center of a child's prayer. As I've gotten older, the "me" is not so important because I know that the relationship with God is there and my prayers of intercession are more along the lines of "Allow me to see what you want me to do in life, help to guide me in what it is that you want me to do." I also don't pray so much for things or for certain events to happen, but rather for larger-scope things, like that the Holy Spirit might work, that we might work as a community together, that we might offer a good witness to the world, that our church may be strengthened, that the clergy and the people will work together. Prayer for me has become much more the prayer of the will of God and the prayer of thanksgiving that He's allowed me so many years in this life to work for His glory and that He hopefully will allow me many more years to work for His glory.

I wouldn't say I have a "favorite" prayer. There's a

prayer that I pray a lot—the Jesus Prayer—that's traditional in the Orthodox church: "O Lord, Jesus Christ, have mercy upon me, a sinner." I used to say that even before I came to seminary, but my seminary training brought it home. I was having some difficulties as a student and I talked to my spiritual father, my father-confessor. He suggested that I add a phrase on to the end that would make the Jesus Prayer not only the Jesus Prayer, but something personal for me that would pull it down from the ethereal, heavenly realm to the earthly realm and make it concrete. So what I said was, "O Lord, Jesus Christ, have mercy upon me, a sinner, and help my thoughts to be in Thee." That way, my thoughts and therefore my activities and actions and the relationships that I have with people are in the presence of God all the time. It doesn't always work, but that's the ideal.

Just this last Sunday was Pentecost, and the *prokimenon*—a short verse that appears before a reading—that we pray at Pentecost is, "Who is so great a God as our God." It epitomizes what it means to be in awe of the great glorification God has given us in this world and what we anticipate in the kingdom to come. The prayer is in anticipation of and hoping that God's mercy will abound and that the things that we have accomplished in this life will stand us in good stead at the Second Coming and at the Judgment, so that we really will inherit the Kingdom of God and have life eternal.

While there's a calming sense to prayer, that's not always the case. Prayer can be energizing and motivating. For me there's a real sense of awe of God about it, and that makes me feel thankful that I'm allowed to participate in creation and be a part of God's plan and His plan for the kingdom. There's this element of joy that all of this has taken place. My favorite Scripture line comes from John 3:16: "For God so loved the world that He gave His only begotten son." He cared enough about us not to leave us hanging, but to take care of us. There's a sense of motherly comfort in that; it's like a shawl being put around your shoulders to keep you warm.

You always get an answer to prayer, but you don't always want to hear the answer. Your ears aren't always open to hearing what He wants to say, and when He does respond, it's not always what you anticipate. As I get older, I've learned to anticipate that that's going to be what happens, and my joy in the answer to my prayer is greater than it was earlier in my life because of the variety of His responses.

The prayer that the Orthodox use most often that encompasses everything liturgically is called the Great Litany. It's at the beginning of the Divine Liturgy, but it also occurs in the other services of the church. It's a series of petitions that are offered up. It begins, "In peace let us pray to the Lord," and the choir sings "Lord, have mercy" after each one of these petitions:

For the peace that is from above and for the salvation of our souls, let us pray to the Lord.

For the peace of the whole world, for the welfare of God's holy churches, and for the union of all, let us pray to the Lord.

For this holy temple, for those who with faith and devoutness and the fear of God have entered therein, let us pray to the Lord.

For our most holy synod of bishops, for our metropolitan, for the diaconate in Christ, for all the clergy and laity, let us pray to the Lord.

These kinds of general prayers that pray for everything have become more of my prayer life in terms of petition. A friend of a friend was getting married and they were writing their own wedding service. They wanted to have some prayers in it. My friend said, "Well, there's nothing better than this Great Litany. We literally pray for everyone: for all the people, for all the churches, for this city, for the holy temple, for every city and land and for those who in faith dwell therein. There's really nothing you can add to this Great Litany." This particular series of petitions say it all in terms of asking for what we need for our life. The last petition is, "Have mercy upon us and keep us, O God, by Thy Grace." All that we're asking for here is to have His mercy given to us and to have Him keep us with Him. It's all by His grace—it's not by our asking—and He gives us this because He is God.

Praying for other people like that has an impact on my relationships with them. If you know that God loves you and that you love God—however broken that relationship can be sometimes on our part—and then you offer up His love in prayer and thanksgiving, then you can't help but love your enemy. But it doesn't always work quite that way. After all, it is a fallen world, and we're not perfect and we will fall and not love our enemy; we will have difficulty with relationships. But when I've had these difficulties, I just place them before God: "I've tried everything I can to work it out, but there's still a difficulty, a disagreement, a dislike; we can't talk to each other." You offer it up to God and you leave it there in His presence and let Him work in your life so that you can change and so that the other person can change. Eventually things will work out. Life changes, people's hearts change, and relationships that were broken before can be fixed.

Prayer life, if it's intense and regular, helps you to deal with those people that you come in contact with who are very angry. When you go to the grocery store and the clerk is really nasty, if you're grounded in a good prayer life, that person will disturb you, but not to the point of making you angry as well. So a good prayer life is a defense against the difficulties that other people are having. Someone can come in the office and yell and scream at you, but you know that they've had a bad day and you look at it from a different point of view because you realize that not everyone is going to offer up everything every day to God.

There are going to be times when we're going to fall and we're going to be angry and we're going to offend and say things that we don't mean. But prayer gives you a greater respect for the person, for the identity of the person in front of you. Rather than treating everyone like numbers or bodies that pass in the day, you want to stop—even if you're very busy—and look on the face of the other person and pay attention. If that person is angry, prayer makes you try to understand why they're angry, to say a word to calm their anger. In the Eastern church we use the word *synergy* to signify the cooperation between God and man that makes the relationship work. There's synergy in the relationship between human beings as well.

Prayer also affects my relationship to the broader community. You realize that the only thing you can do for people sometimes is to pray. It's one of my pet peeves that people say to someone who's lost a relative or has an illness in the family, "I can't help you or do anything, so I'll pray for you," as if prayer were the last resort. Prayer should be the *first* resort. The first thing you do is pray, and then you take action, if at all possible. This element of prayer helps to unite people in the world. I may never meet a person from Bosnia, but I'll have a tie in my heart to them because I've prayed for them and I've prayed with them. I know they're praying to God for His intercession in their situation. There's no question but that prayer is a common element, and it's not just among Christians.

REMBERT G. WEAKLAND, O.S.B.

Rembert G. Weakland, O.S.B., a Benedictine monk, was named archbishop of Milwaukee's Catholic Archdiocese by Pope Paul VI in 1977. Before that he was abbot primate of the International Benedictine Confederation. He was chairman of the committee of U.S. bishops that wrote the 1986 pastoral letter on the economy, Economic Justice for All. *He has chaired bishops' committees on liturgy and ecumenical and interreligious affairs, and is cochair of the committee on dialogue with the Eastern Orthodox churches. He received a papal appointment to the Commission for Implementing the* Constitution on the Sacred Liturgy *of the Second Vatican Council. Archbishop Weakland is an accomplished pianist who studied music at the Juilliard School of Music and Columbia University.*

To me prayer is just being aware of the presence of God in one's life. It's a conscious awareness, when you tune in to His presence.

Being a Benedictine, I've had to learn to do this in different ways. One of the hardest points of my life was changing from being a Benedictine monk to being a bishop. As a monk, it was wonderful to have a period of time set aside when nobody could interrupt you—no phones could go off, nothing. Now I don't have that same kind of rhythm each day; I don't have the same kind of time that I had as a monk. I have to learn to accept that and use the time that I do have. That's why I now pray shorter prayers throughout the day; I take advantage of all kinds of opportunities. What I tell high school kids at their confirmation is to get some gimmicks that help you to pray. For example, Saint Teresa of Avila used to say she would pray when the bell in the clock tower would ring. So what I do is say a prayer every time I open the refrigerator door; when you live alone, you find yourself opening the refrigerator door an enormous number of times during the day! It's just one of those things that helps you to think of God's presence.

I find that when I'm watching TV, commercials provide a great time in which to pray—especially during the last minutes of any basketball game, where there are so many commercials, you pray up a storm. I like to pray when I get on my Nordictrack, and when I do things regularly, day after day. I even tell people to pray every time you push the button to open the garage door. If you're taking those moments, then you're praying throughout the day. They're all simple reminders of God's presence, and you don't have to go through a lot of words. As a bishop, with my more hectic schedule, I find myself using these reminders a lot more than I ever did as a monk years ago.

But I can't get completely out of my good old monastic routine. I find that I do need the Liturgy of the Hours. I need something in the morning and something in the evening that tunes me in to the Liturgy. The Liturgy of the Hours is a stable kind of prayer form that goes way back. First of all it divides the year into its normal seasons of Advent, the Christmas cycle, the Lenten cycle, the Easter cycle, and the ordinary times during the summer. It's a way of taking all of the great mysteries of the life of Jesus Christ and spreading them out through the whole year, so that one has a chance to reflect on the whole of who Jesus Christ was and is. Then each day is divided so that you have morning, noon, and evening prayer. It gives you a chance to take the time of the day and divide it and make sure that the presence of Christ that is so much of Eucharist stays with you throughout the whole day.

The Liturgy is composed mostly of: psalms; good old prayers that have nurtured thousands of people throughout history; readings from the Old Testament; Patristic readings; New Testament readings; and then prayers and hymns that keep one in tune with the season. To me this has been a wealth of prayers that I just have to have, not only because of its background but because it keeps me in tune with what's going on in the church season.

So I find the Liturgy of the Hours is still very strong in my life. This might seem strange, but as a bishop I pray it more slowly than I had as a monk. I guess then when it's a duty, you try to get it over with. Now I do it more slowly, and sometimes I stop in the middle of the Liturgy in the midst of a psalm, and try to resay the psalm in my own words. I take a standard prayer and try to redo it in my own words, to make sure that the prayer is mine. That slows me down a lot, and I find it very helpful.

On the other hand I do have to be frank and say that I am not scrupulous about keeping the Liturgy of the Hours. So, for example, if I'm out and have a big Mass ceremony somewhere in the evening, I don't feel the obligation to then say a few Liturgy of the Hours words. To me the Mass was what God gave me for that evening, and that's enough for me. I don't worry too much about the mechanical idea that you have to say so many words in a day.

I've also had to learn, as a bishop, that wherever I was, I had to make the liturgy very important to me. It's hard to describe, but the first year I kind of rebelled at having to be out every night for confirmation in the springtime; it was like having too many banquets and dinners liturgically. Now I've come to say to myself, "Well, even if it's confirmation night, that's fine. That's what the Lord's giving me. I have to take these young people here and their enthusiasm and their prayer and make it mine and be enriched by it." Each group of people who are praying out there is different, and their prayer is important for my prayer. So I've relaxed a bit about that aspect of my life as a bishop.

And I have to admit that twenty or thirty years ago most of my prayer life would have consisted of petitions. Now it is much less so. I will pray for things that people ask me to pray for. When it comes to myself, I find myself just being aware of God's presence, trying to relax in His presence, trying to be thankful in my heart—without at the same time asking for a lot of stuff. Maybe I'll get into a crisis where I'll really have to whip up a storm again with prayers of petition, but right now it's not a great part of my prayer life.

Not getting answer to prayers doesn't even bother me much. Like everybody else, I've got a little bit of that Italian way about me; if I don't get what I want, goodbye to that saint. The Italians do that. When they don't get what they want, they take it out on the saint. I have a little bit of that. Or I do what everybody else does: pray like mad to get through something, make all these promises, and then two minutes later, forget all about it.

I have both Christ and the Holy Spirit in mind most of the time when I pray. I believe so strongly in that theology of indwelling and baptism, of being conformed to Christ. I'm very impressed—and this hit me years ago—that no prayer reaches the throne of God the Father except in and through Jesus Christ and as the Spirit gives it to you. That has been very powerful in my life and in my prayer life. The same prayer that I might utter opening a refrigerator door is as much through Christ and in the Spirit as celebrating Mass; from Christ's point of view, it's the same. I don't really pray to God the Father, I don't know why not. I know that at liturgy all prayers are offered up to God the Father, but I guess I'm a little bit more sentimental, and somehow Jesus Christ is very real to me.

During those moments when I open refrigerator doors or car doors, I fall back almost entirely on the Jesus Prayer—simply, "Lord Jesus Christ, have mercy on me" or "Lord Jesus Christ, I love you." I always make it in two parts; that's the way one does it with one's breathing. But sometimes I don't even say that; I'm just aware of Christ's presence and let it go at that. I also have come, when I pray, always to think of Christ as being within me. I would have to say that I'm very Christocentric, sometimes Spiritcentric, and always interiorized, not outside of me.

I also try to take a little bit of time every day for something more like meditation. On retreat, or if I have a day off, I take a walk in the woods and fall into a more intense kind of prayer for a longer period of time than usual. I fall back on that kind of meditation without text, if you will, and I find it very calming, very nourishing. There are times—I would have to admit that I don't ask for them, and they're rare—where I think it also could become a bit more emotional, if that's the right word, a bit more experiential. I always get a little nervous about that whole area, though, and I think that one can dupe oneself into thinking that that's great prayer. So I'm cautious.

I used to do a lot of yoga, and I found that body positions and that kind of experience was a good one. After talking to Dom Bede Griffith, the Benedictine, I tried to integrate that kind of more quietude in the breathing and the body posture with the more Christocentric kind of praying. This was about thirty years ago, when I went through what you might call my Buddhist-Hindu period. Out of that I gained a great respect for the Catholic tradition that comes out of the Jesus Prayer and things of this sort. But I also have to be honest and say I'm a little leery of playing psychological tricks with myself. I enjoy meditation—I do feel more relaxed, and the breathing aspects and all that are helpful—but I guess I'm sensitive to not trying to think that the calmer I am, the more psychologically relaxed I am, that therefore the better my prayer is. That kind of thinking makes me nervous.

I always remember that the late Cardinal John Henry Newman said he always thought he was making great strides in the illuminative way, until he got migraine headaches and realized that sometimes they're simply physical things and not necessarily God's presence each time. So if there's a day in which I find myself overwhelmed with problems and can't get my mind onto anything, and I don't come away feeling calm and relaxed or on an emotional high, I try to tell myself that nevertheless maybe my prayer was okay. That's as much as this bishop could do on this day; "Lord, you've got to take me as I am." I find the same thing when I'm with charismatic renewal people; I get very nervous when they try to evaluate prayer through the measurement of the emotional involvement.

I have always been convinced that there is a relationship between the aesthetic experience and the prayer experience. Sometimes I really can't distinguish whether some of the deepest kind of prayer moments for me are aesthetic high moments or prayer high moments. I'll never forget when I was in first-year high school hearing Schubert's Fifth Symphony; to me it was a religious experience. Sometimes that also happens in my travels, when I've seen something that's just overwhelming in its beauty or I hear a great piece of music.

After I've listened to music like that or prayed, I have a sense of well-being that comes from that feeling that in spite of all your faults and failings and inabilities, God is there. That is calming, it is helpful. Also, when you get into a job like mine where you don't have answers most of the time, you have to somehow put it in somebody's hands. Sometimes I come away feeling, "Well, that's all I can do, just hand it over so it is God's now." I have to do that especially with personnel issues, because you just don't know how it's going to work out. If I have someone coming to see me and I am nervous about it, knowing that if I say the wrong thing, I could do a lot of damage to that person, I'll say a little prayer to the Holy Spirit for light and guidance on how to handle it before the person comes into the room. About the only time I pray for guidance is from the Holy Spirit, although I don't do it too much; I do it on an ad hoc basis.

I have a hard time being Mother Teresa. I wish that I could look at every poor person out on the street and say that I can see Christ in them. But I don't find it easy to look at street people or people sitting in the gutter and find Christ in them. I guess I've got to do that a little bit more self-consciously and try harder. I wish it would come more easily to me. You read these lives of people like Dorothy Day and Mother Teresa, and I wonder, are they doing psychological gymnastics or what?

I try to find Christ in everybody, but sometimes it's a search. It's not sufficient to me to say God loves that person and God loves that person just as much as God loves you, et cetera. I try to do that, but I've always had a hard time with that whole theology of finding Christ in everybody. Saint Benedict's rule expects you to find Christ in the Superior, and that's often tough. You're even supposed to find Christ in the guests that knock at the door. I think the reason being was that, in those days, when a guest would knock at the door, you had to deprive yourself of food or whatever to take care of them, and that would take a certain sacrifice. For that reason you would have to see Christ in them. But I've never found this to be real easy; it all seemed a bit like psychologically playing games. Maybe I should take that up sometime with someone a little more in tune with it. I try to look at people who are hurting, who are out there on the street; I try to say that those people have a worth and a dignity in the eyes of God as much as I do, and see their potential, but I find it hard to say they're Christ.

Prayer does affect my relationship to other people, though. I think the reason is that when one takes time out to pray, especially at a moment of difficult personal relationships, it forces you to be honest yourself. I think it's impossible to pray—especially over a long period of time, especially with a certain quietude—without having to face reality as it is. For me that has been very helpful, because if you get into a sensitive relationship where you think you've been hurt, or whatever, and you pull back from it and pray over it, you usually find that maybe there *was* a grain of truth there. Prayer has helped me to make sure that I'm not overreacting or reacting insensibly, and to pull back a bit from hurts and things, put them in a proper perspective, and then have the kind of courage that one needs to move ahead to face the situation and move on.

LISA WOOD

Lisa Wood is a partner in the Boston law firm of Nutter, McClennen and Fish, where she has worked since earning her law degree from Boston College Law School in 1984. She works on child-abuse issues for the Boston courts and is often appointed guardian ad litem for abused or neglected children with special educational needs. A member of Saint Paul's Episcopal Church in Dedham, Massachusetts, she is active in the Junior League of Boston, the Boston Bar Association, and the National Conference of Christians and Jews. She and her husband, Peter Michelson, live with their daughter, Marissa Lie, and their dog, Anna, in Medfield, Massachusetts.

I think about prayer in two different ways. One I call formal prayer, which is praying in church. I'm an Episcopalian, so that means following our Prayer Book for Morning Prayer or Holy Communion with a group of people in church. We follow a schedule of prayers and ritual behavior that's pretty much the same from Sunday to Sunday, and from holy days to holy days. It's a structure that I'm familiar with and that I've known for years.

Then there's another form that I think of as private prayer, where in the midst of church or just in the midst of my daily life I might stop and pray. It's usually the result of two extreme emotions, either extreme happiness—I might stop just to thank God for blessings—or extreme sadness, when something awful has happened, and I stop just to try to pull myself together. I do pro bono work on child-abuse cases, and there are times when the information I learn is so horrific that I need to stop and pray for a moment. An example of the opposite extreme might be when I take in a sight of natural beauty. For example, at our vacation place in northern Michigan I watch the sun come up over the lake, and at such times I usually end up saying a prayer of thanksgiving.

There are times in my life when I seem to engage in silent prayer daily, and there are times when that might only happen once a week. I engage in formal prayer pretty much once a week. Sometimes it's just Holy Communion or Morning Prayer on Sundays, sometimes it's a prayer group with other members of my parish held during the week. But on average it would be about once a week for formal prayer. When there are religious holidays, I increase my formal and private prayers quite a bit. Typically at these times my family is together more, and there are more opportunities when I want to give a prayer of thanksgiving.

To understand why the Episcopal Prayer Book is so important to me, it's helpful to understand my background. I was raised in a fairly religious household, and my father is now a bishop in the Episcopal church. When I was growing up, he was a deacon and then a priest in the Episcopal church. My mother is an Episcopalian as well, although she was raised a Baptist. I went to church regularly from a young age. We moved around quite a bit. If I look back at my childhood, the one experience that remained the same even though we lived in dramatically different neighborhoods—sometimes inner-city, sometimes rural—was going to church every Sunday. Even though the churches and the communities in which we worshiped varied dramatically, the service was virtually the same. The Prayer Book was modernized in the Sixties—there used to be a Book of Common Prayer from 1928—but even with those changes the services have stayed remarkably similar.

As I've gotten older, participation in formal worship in an Episcopal church has offered more comfort to me. I think this is in part because the experience of formal worship brings back my childhood and is a great source of familiarity. It pulls together a lot of things and provides a real sense of continuity. On a larger scale I also realize that people have been standing or kneeling together for hundreds of years, saying virtually the same prayers, both within the larger Anglican community and among Christians as a whole. For example I have had an opportunity to travel overseas and realize that the Episcopal Prayer Book is not dissimilar to what Anglicans across the world say. I went to a Catholic high school, and there are a number of similarities between the Catholic Eucharist and Holy Communion service. So when standing in formal prayer, I'm reminded that all Christians around the world are saying the same thing. That's an important image for me to hold on to. It underscores for me the strength of Christianity and what we, as Christians, might be able to accomplish toward the goal we share of making the world a better place.

Morning Prayer is a form of service in the Episcopal Prayer Book that is used when you're not going to have Holy Communion, when you're not going to share the bread and the wine. There are a couple of different versions. It's mostly spoken prayer, and there are some long prayers that the priest and the congregation say together. There's a long series I like very much where the priest says one line and the parish responds with another. It tends to be a "lower" service, more informal, and with less ritual, than Holy Communion. Not all Episcopalians celebrate Holy Communion every Sunday. This seems particularly so in New England, where the low church is much more typical. Apparently having communion every week would be considered very high-church. It's very common in this part of the country to have communion only on the first and third Sundays of the month and to have Morning Prayer the other Sundays. My dad's now a bishop in Michigan, and when I go out there, I notice that having Holy Communion every week is much more typical. I guess it varies from region to region. I like the words said during Morning Prayer, but I get a great sense of strength from receiving communion. One thing interesting that we've done in my church is for those who want to have communion every week, we have a short Eucharist service after Morning Prayer. Probably about twenty or twenty-five members of the parish go up to the front of the church where we have a choir stall and altar, and one of the two priests ministering the service that day gives Holy Communion and goes through the Holy Communion service in addition to Morning Prayer.

If I had to pick one thing that draws me to the Episcopal Church, I'd say that I enjoy a high church. Usually you associate a high church with more ritual, and the ritual aspect of prayer is very important to me. It's hard for me to know whether it's just the familiarity of the ritual or whether I find it easier to pray in that context. The higher the church, the more I feel a presence of spirituality. For example, when a church uses incense and a sung Mass, I feel the presence of God more strongly.

I should also say that sung prayer is extremely important to me. When singing hymns or other prayers in the church, I feel as though I am offering a gift of beauty to God. The beauty of the music always manages to lift my spirits. Growing up, I often sang in church choirs. My mother also did, and I have fond memories of her practicing at home on the piano. I am now trying to teach my daughter, who is two and a half, about Christianity by teaching her spirituals. I want to communicate the strength that early Afro-Americans drew from singing spirituals, as well as the basic Bible lessons communicated in their songs. I sing to her almost every night, and she is picking up the spirituals very quickly. The other night she started singing "We Are Climbing Jacob's Ladder" on her own initiative. I'd only sung it to her twice before. It is very important that she be raised with religion and participate in formal worship on a weekly basis, because the same experience was very important to my husband's and my own development of values and moral fiber.

Because my religion is so tied in with community and a sense of community responsibility, the idea of praying together with a group is very important to me too. As a teenager I worked at an Episcopal church camp, and the counselors used to get together for reunions and whatnot and hold what are called *agape* meals. It's somewhat like an informal Eucharist. We wrote our own service, baked bread, and had wine and an open time for prayer. On the first and third Wednesday of the month my church has a meeting in downtown Boston for those of us who work downtown. We meet for Bible study and read what's called the daily office, which is another prayer service in the Prayer Book. We say a prayer, read a reading from the Bible, say a few more prayers, and then while we're eating lunch discuss the reading. I also pray in groups when we're saying grace at mealtime. There are times when I might share either a prayer of thanksgiving or one seeking forgiveness with a family member if we've experienced something together that's made me have one of those two feelings. And I sometimes feel that people are praying jointly when they are spending time together talking about how to make this world a better place, acknowledging that they all feel that that's important and it's their responsibility.

Probably my strongest religious tenet has to do with what responsibilities I feel while living this life and not with that aspect of Christianity that has to do with what might happen in the hereafter. I try to remind myself of my responsibility as a Christian to make this world a better place by going to church regularly and by being involved in the community. When I am involved and see horrible things happening, or see great things happening, I seek prayer with God. As I mentioned earlier, I've worked on child-abuse cases for years. In the children I've worked with I've seen a lot, and I feel awe and wonder at the beauty of their life and their strength of character. I get spiritual strength from these children. As I get older, I think this work is more and more a part of my own spirituality, my own religious beliefs. My parents are very committed to civil rights and social justice through their commitment to the church, so I think that I'm connected to that part of my family heritage. There's something about the discipline of going to church and saying the prayers and listening to what they say that helps me be disciplined about being involved in the community and always trying to do something for those less fortunate. The more I do the community work, the richer my own religious experience of church is every Sunday; the two feed each other.

Going to church every week, listening to sermons, and having moments of contemplation force me to think more about what my responsibilities are in my daily life. I would hope that prayer makes me deal with people more effectively, more kindly, more generously than I might do otherwise. I'm a trial lawyer, so I'm always dealing with conflict, and there are times when that can get the best of you. One of the prayers both in the Morning

Prayer and Holy Communion services involves saying that you have sinned and asking for forgiveness. I try to review what I might have done recently that I could have done better.

In general I'm both delighted and horrified by the human condition, and I try through prayer to see the best in everyone and treat everyone that I deal with with respect. I also try as much as possible to do what I can to help when I see bad things happening to a particular individual. That affects my dealings in work and my dealings with anybody. I try to treat everyone with respect, and that includes the parents or other alleged perpetrators of child abuse, with whom I interact all the time in my cases.

In my prayer I feel as though I'm looking for strength to be a better Christian. I've never felt a particular answer, any words or sign coming back, although I do believe that that happens for some people. I have had family members and friends who have had personal problems, and I went through a period when I sought strength to deal better with those and have more courage. I did gain more strength through prayer, but it wasn't so much that someone answered back and told me, "Yes, you should do this." The process each week of reminding myself that I'm going to be responsible and treat all with whom I interact with respect is a way of keeping me disciplined and on track; I feel as though someone is listening and that I'm being watched, so I need to be honest. I cannot fool whomever it is I pray to.

SIMILARITIES OF PRAYER

These conversations about prayer with more than two dozen Americans prompt three surprising thoughts. One is almost amusing: There is hardly any human activity—including getting up in the morning, exercising, working, driving, eating, having sex, going to the bathroom, reading, watching television, talking to people, going to bed at night, and waking up in the middle of the night—that someone doesn't associate with prayer. People who pray *do* seem to "pray without ceasing."

The second reaction is not amusing at all; in fact it's quite sobering. As people talk about their prayer lives, they talk about their toughest experiences—not only their own illnesses but the serious illnesses and deaths of spouses, children, and parents. Prayer isn't a game or a hobby; it's something that people turn to in order to get through the things that seem impossible to get through.

The third reaction is that despite prayer's power and presence, so many people who pray have not analyzed their own prayer lives. Prayer comes from the gut; we don't always understand it, we just do it.

Many people even had trouble defining prayer. Some, like High Star and Ron Nakasone, come from traditions that reject the notion of prayer to a God outside the world. But they engage in rituals and meditation that serve a purpose almost identical to that of prayer, in that they carry on a conversation with a power outside themselves, even if that power is life itself. So sometimes the

lines between Western and non-Western ways of spirituality are not always easy to identify.

"Conversation" is clearly the most popular metaphor
that people use to describe prayer. That metaphor of
conversation is particularly interesting because many
people are not sure exactly who or what is on the other
side of the conversation. For example, Dan Seals says, "I
don't claim to know God, and I don't think anybody on
this earth can say, 'Yeah, I know God and I get through
all the time.' I think that this great power that made us
all is unknowable and can't be sensed from the outer
senses."

The Christian belief in the Holy Trinity—Father, Son,
and Holy Spirit—seems to provide Christians with the
opportunity to pray to the different parts of God that
match their needs. They might, for example, offer thanks
to the Father, talk to Jesus about their problems, and ask
the Holy Spirit for inspiration. Catholics offer even more
options; Jane Redmont and Sidney Callahan describe the
importance of prayers to Mary, the Mother of Jesus, while
Mary Frances Robles often prays to Saint Jude, one of an
array of saints that Catholics associate with different
needs. Rajshri Gopal describes a similar approach among
Hindus, who pray both to one God and to many gods.

Yet "conversation" does not exhaust people's descrip-
tions of prayer. Several also use some form of the word
contact or *connection*. Carol Mu'min talks of a contact
that feels "like an electrical charge," while Dan Seals describes the hair on his arms standing up and the feeling
that his heart is getting larger inside his body. Sandra
Clopine describes a feeling of contact so overwhelming
that she prostrates herself on the floor, and Larry
Kushner says he feels that "God is the ocean and I am
the wave." The feeling of connection for many people
relates to a prayer of oneness with life.

Finally, there is widespread belief that prayer is a part of life, not something apart from daily life. For example, High Star says, "I would say that living is a prayer. To live each day is a prayer in the sense that it's an expression of God. It's the total being that you are, and whether it's spiritual, intellectual, physical, or emotional, it's still the process of living. If you choose dark thoughts, bad thoughts, you're still praying, but you're praying for the dark element as opposed to the light element. The whole process of thinking is actually a prayer because what you hold in your thoughts is what you bring into the world."

That's very close to Robert Schuller's belief that "the highest level [of prayer] would be the actions I take that bless people. I pay attention, I care about them, I listen to them, I feel for them. And in the process of being that kind of a caring human being, I am praying at the highest level. Prayer at the highest level is glorifying God, and I glorify God when I become a really generous and caring person."

These definitions of prayer explain why people pray. Sidney Callahan says, "If you ask what my prayer is about, it consists mostly of 'Help!' and 'Thank you.'" If prayer is directed toward a force outside of ourselves, then we invoke it when we feel things are out of control, and often we offer prayers of thanksgiving even at difficult times. Norman Lear, for all his fame and fortune, is thankful for cool sheets in the middle of the night and a clean ceiling to look at first thing in the morning. Robert Schuller finds reason for thanks even in times of tragedy. "My daughter lost her leg in a terrible motorcycle accident. When I heard, the prayer that I said was a thank-you. Thank you, God, that she's alive. Thank you, God, that she just lost one leg. Thank you, God, that her face wasn't smashed. Thank you that her brain wasn't injured. Thank you that they got her to the hospital. At those times that's the only way to pray."

Still, several types of prayer fall outside the range of "Help" and "Thank you." Some prayers are prayers for acceptance and understanding, while others, such as Sandra Clopine's prostration before her God, express awe and wonderment. Larry Kushner describes his reaction to a simple blessing before a meal: "The one that I recite the most frequently which, after having recited it ten thousand times, means much more than the simple words, is translated from the Hebrew 'Holy One of Blessing, Your presence fills creation, You bring forth this bread from the earth.' I try to recite that before every meal. When it works, I all of a sudden realize, just for a second, 'Oh, my God, I didn't make this food. I don't know how this food got here. I really am dumbfounded before the experience of my own sustenance, my own nourishment. I don't understand how it is that I'm able to stay alive."

Many people can't remember a time when prayer wasn't important in their lives. Even those who changed their religious affiliation as adults recall prayer as important when they were children. Others describe prayer becoming more important in their early teens or college years. But whenever prayer first became important, virtually everyone reports changes in their prayer lives, some of which involve the content of prayer. For example, Archbishop Weakland says he is less likely to ask for things in prayer than he did when he was younger. Others report finding greater comfort in prayer. Carol Mu'min says it becomes easier to "make contact" with God; and George Gallup says, "the more I pray, the more I want to."

How do people pray? Most use a mix of spontaneous and set prayers. Spontaneous prayers are the most personal conversations with God. Those are the ones in which you ask for help for your family, express thanks for your blessings, or look for inspiration for your work. Not surprisingly, those who come from more liturgical traditions are more likely to use some set prayers as well. Eve Rudin says she likes the feeling that Jews all over the world, as they have been throughout history, are saying the same prayers. Her reaction is similar to that of Lisa Wood, who enjoys the fact that Anglicans and many other Christians around the world use almost identical prayers. Larry Kushner even believes there's nothing to add to the existing prayer script. And many, such as Marlene Payne and Carol Mu'min, like the comfort of repeating prayers that have been around as long as family members and old friends.

Most people, even those with a less liturgical tradition, have favorite prayers. The Lord's Prayer, the prayer of Saint Francis of Assisi, the Episcopal Book of Common Prayer, the Serenity Prayer, and the Jesus Prayer are a favorite means of expression for many of those interviewed.

People also use very short, set prayers. Jews use the many *berakhas*, or blessings that, Kushner says, "begin with the phrase 'Praised are You, Lord our God, King of the universe who . . .' and then you fill in the blank." Catholics use brief "ejaculatory" prayers such as Weakland's use of the Jesus Prayer, "Lord Jesus Christ, have mercy on me." Campbell and Redmont pay tribute to the black-church tradition of saying "Thank you, Jesus" at appropriate points during the day. These short prayers provide an opportunity for contact in the middle of a hectic day.

Some form of meditation is fairly popular as part of prayer, but its description varies. Some do use the repetition of a phrase to bring on a sense of calm. Others describe times of silence and stillness that include elements of meditation but not the repetition of a single phrase. Evangelicals simply use *meditation* to describe a time of serious reflection about a subject such as a Bible passage. And all emphasize the importance of slow, deep breathing.

People pray at any time throughout the day, but some patterns do emerge. For many it's important to pray early in the morning; Martin Marty pinpoints his prayer at "5:59 A.M." every day. Prayer in the morning gives some people a clear head and a chance to set their priorities for the day. Similarly, many people take stock in prayer at the end of the day.

Exercise turns out to be a popular time for prayer: Foster and Schuller pray while they jog; Weakland prays while using his Nordictrack machine; Lear has Saint Francis of Assisi's prayer taped to his treadmill; and Callahan prays while playing tennis or sitting in the sauna. Exercise seems to provide two elements helpful to prayer: mental privacy and regular breathing.

Saying grace at meals is still important to many, and Gallup has practically made it a cause: "I always say grace at meals now, and I do this in public because I think it's a good witness. People are sort of stunned and stare at you in disbelief, but I think it's a good thing to do."

Music and the arts also help many people pray. Greeley says music and poetry spark prayer in him; he calls writing his own poetry a form of prayer. Weakland claims the first time he heard Schubert's Fifth Symphony was a religious experience, and Redmont says she was converted by Mozart's Requiem. Marty says the prayerful state he enters while listening to classical music helped him cope with his first wife's death. High Star says, "Everything is done through music in our tradition; music is our connection to the spirit world."

Stories are important, too. Greeley uses stories as

homilies when celebrating Mass. Seals talks about the movie *Resurrection*, Kushner quotes from *Little Big Man*, and Marty uses a comic strip—"Pogo"—as an inspiration for prayer.

Reading is also associated with prayer. Some people pray while reading the Bible or immediately afterward. Others read spiritual literature as an aid to prayer. Some write about the thoughts that come to them in prayer. Greeley keeps a daily journal; Gallup collects prayers in a notebook; and many of Marty's writings are born in his "hitchhiking" on the spiritual writings of others.

Some religious traditions place more emphasis than others on worship services, and it shouldn't be surprising that people who belong to more liturgical traditions place more value on prayer at weekly services. All of the Catholics in this book emphasize the role of the Mass. Lisa Wood's prayer life revolves around the Episcopal Morning Prayer and Holy Communion services. Martin Marty gets an anchor in the Lutheran service. Marlene Payne spends three hours each Sunday in Mormon services. Silk goes to services twice a day. For these people services provide two major elements: a familiar liturgy, and a connection to other people who share the same religious beliefs.

Most people report that prayer gives them a sense of calm or a sense of peace. Callahan says, "Prayer always makes me feel wonderful, because it makes me feel more alive, or more spirited, or more happy, or more energized, or more peaceful. It immediately opens up the world to me." Gallup says, "I feel empowered. Sometimes I feel as if I'm on a high. . . . Prayer gives me a sense of peace now and the assurance of future peace, even after death. I feel confirmed and empowered." Robles comments, "Prayer makes me feel a little at ease, that [God] is listening. There's no sign right off the bat that He hears me, but I know He's listening, and that makes me feel comfortable."

But prayer isn't always calming. Seals reports, "The way I feel after prayer depends upon the situation. If I pray for another individual who's very sick, I sometimes still carry the agitation of worry within me afterward." Jane Redmont admits, "I have a fairly stormy inner life much of the time, but that doesn't bother me because I know it's a part of the contemplative life. It's a part of having a relationship with God—or, if you don't want to talk about it in those terms, part of any experience of sitting in mediation. You're always going to run into your own inner turmoil. At this point in my life I just kind of say 'Hi' to it when I encounter it, because I know it's par for the course in the spiritual life."

Not everyone has a dramatic story about a prayer experience, but many do:

• Phil Bom recalls how the prayers of a supporting community gave him and his wife the strength to cope with the death of their son.

• Sidney Callahan recalls the Virgin Mary appearing to tell her that she would be cured of her illness.

• Sandra Clopine describes feelings of awe that leave her prostrate before her God.

• Richard Foster describes an incident in which God taught him "Sabbath prayer."

• Carole Mu'min says she is often so overcome with awe as she begins to pray that she can barely speak.

• Marlene Payne describes her sense that her Heavenly Father folded His wings around her and gave her peace and comfort.

• Jane Redmont describes feelings of healing at an interfaith AIDS service.

• Dan Seals recalls an encounter in Israel with a force that was loving and frightening at the same time.

All in all, the people in this book reveal an amazing amount of similarities in the way they pray and the way they feel about prayer. But the issue that reveals the most *division* is the question of whether and how their prayers are answered.

Some people feel that it isn't right to ask for things in prayer. Lear says, "I would never consider praying to ask for anything, either for myself or for anybody else. All I can expect of it is to let me serve, to be the kind of person who can give as close to 100 percent of myself as I can." Similarly High Star and Nakasone don't believe in prayers of petition or supplication. Robles remembers, "My Mom was the one who taught us how to pray. She told us not to ask for material things, for they weren't important."

Martin Marty is both passionate and eloquent in rejecting what he terms as "offensive" prayer: "I find the most offensive kind of prayer to be when 250 Marines get killed in Lebanon and 4 survive and their families go on television and say, 'Well, we really prayed, and so they were spared.' That's an unbiblical game, it's magic, it's superstition. . . . You don't hear about this kind of magic from people who are in this regular conversation with God; you hear it most from people who think they've got God figured out. They had been very remote and then they phase into prayer on their lucky day; they win the lottery. Then they say, 'I prayed about these bills and then God gave it to me.' No, God didn't give you anything, God didn't rig that lottery; *it just happened.* To me theology and prayer are what we do with what just happened, what interpretation we put on them, what attitudes we have toward them."

Others believe they receive direct answers to prayer, and describe concrete results. Ann Garvin and Rajshri Gopal both see answers to prayers when they find an object that they've lost. But most describe answers to prayers that are far more subtle. At one level they believe prayers are answered when they feel less suffering. Gopal says simply, "I get answers to prayer when my suffering goes away." Others find answers when they have new insights or find solutions to problems. Robert Schuller says, "I know I've gotten an answer when I feel it and I know it." Ann Garvin reports, "A time [comes] when all of a sudden I know exactly what I'm supposed to do or what was missing."

Two of the people in this book both say prayers answered in the deaths of their grandfathers. Eve Rudin says, "It wasn't an answer to a specific prayer, but I felt God's presence in that there was just some justice in it. He had had the opportunity to live a full life." Dan Seals, sixteen when his grandfather died, commented, "My grandfather was dying of cancer, and I was down on my knees in my innocence praying to Jesus to save him and bring him back and cure the cancer so that he could be with me longer. . . . They said when he died he was smiling, looking up at the ceiling and smiling. It sounds like he was going to a wonderful place if it made Grand-dad smile. He liked what was fixin' to happen to him. He was healed, although it wasn't in the way I thought it was going to be."

Seals's reminiscence strikes another common theme: the belief that while God's answers to prayers may not necessarily be what we want, they still have meaning. Sandra Clopine encountered despair when her husband tragically died as a young missionary in Africa, but finds meaning in the fact that his death inspired a number of Africans to enter the Christian ministry. Joan Campbell remarks, "God never answers our prayers in a direct way; cause and effect are not immediate in prayer. Now, as I look back over my life, I can say that my prayers *have* been answered. One of my prayers has always been that I might have a meaningful life, that I might have a full life, that I might be given things to do that make a difference.... I look back over my life [and see that] I've been guided substantially in my life into the things I have done, and they do weave something of a tapestry that makes sense. As I look back over my life, I can see a way in which my prayers have been answered, although it's not the way I would have designed it. And I think once you get older, you say, 'And thank God that I wasn't allowed to design it.' I have a much better life for having been guided than if I had myself been able, every step of the way, to do what I thought was the right thing to do."

But even when people ask God for help, they still accept their own responsibility to do all that they can as well. Marlene Payne feels, "It's much easier to pray when you're trying to live in tune with your principles. I feel like, 'I've done my part, now please do your part.'" Similarly Carole Mu'min says, "I also understand prayer goes hand in hand with work. In Islam you don't pray and just sit there." And Joan Campbell recalls her father's words: "I was not a very big kid when he said, 'Let me tell you about prayer. If you're on the railroad track, and you are tied down, and the train is coming, pray to God that that train will stop. If you are on the railroad track and you are not tied down, don't pray to God; get up and move off the track if the train is coming.'"

So it's clear that when we pray, we also call on ourselves to do more than we've done, to do things differently or with new energy. We pray not just to move God; we also pray to move ourselves.

Much of what people say about prayer concerns their internal attitudes and changes. But they also describe how prayer changes the way they relate to other people, their work, and the world around them. Almost everyone interviewed says that prayer puts life into "perspective" and improves their relationships with other people. Billy Graham says, "I find myself praying while I'm talking to people. I say, 'Lord, help me to say the right thing,' and 'Lord, help me not to be offensive; help me to say the thing that will encourage people to believe.'" Marlene Payne reflects, "[Prayer] helps me to see people in a more compassionate light and to forgive. I pray to have a much more peaceful and tolerant attitude toward my husband. I mean, I love him anyway, but it just helps keep the tone of the marriage much sweeter; it helps me to let go of the little irritations that come up."

Carole Mu'min comments, "I'm fortunate in that my husband is also a praying man. Early on in our marriage when we wouldn't see eye to eye, he would be the one who would say, 'Let's say a prayer over this.' Now, there you are in the middle of a healthy discussion (as we call them), when suddenly you stop and pray for guidance or whatever. I attribute *that* to why our marriage is together today. When you come up out of prayer, it puts everything in perspective. I certainly agree with those who say 'A family that prays together stays together.'" And Richard Foster says, "People who really pray—not people who just analyze prayer or dissect it, but who actually do it—become more loving, more sensitive to other people. I've watched this happen, and I think I'm reflecting not only my own experience but the experience of many other people. Prayer enlarges our ability to embrace other people."

For many, prayer leads to some form of social action beyond merely praying for things to happen. Foster goes on to say, "Of necessity, love of God eventuates in love of neighbor. The two great commandments are really one. Prayer *always* has a social dimension to it. Prayer, to be real prayer, does not take us out of the world; it sends us into the world and excites our endeavors to heal the world."

It's a cliché to say that prayer is the greatest untapped power in the world; it's also true that we can pray for evil as well as for good. But these interviews offer strong evidence that, on balance, we're all a little better off when people pray.

Postscript: The Reflection Response, or the Five Habits of Highly Effective Pray-ers

Dr. Herbert Benson has identified the "Relaxation Response" as a generic form of meditation found in most religions and in some secular belief systems. He found that when people sit in a comfortable position, close their eyes, relax their muscles, breathe slowly and naturally, and repeat a short phrase—such as "One," "Om," or "Shalom"—for about twenty minutes, they create beneficial physical changes in their bodies. These include lowered heart rate, decreased breathing rate, lowered blood pressure, slower brain waves, and slower metabolism.

A number of the people interviewed for this book showed common use of Relaxation Response–like behaviors. But there is more to prayer than meditation. For virtually everyone in this book there is an intellectual side of prayer, an active reflection on themselves, their world, and their most basic values and beliefs. While some people see meditation as seeking stillness, others see meditation as active reflection about a subject. Don't just stop and smell the roses; stop and think about the roses.

It's become clear that prayer includes a *Reflection* Response as well as a Relaxation Response, and just as everyone can benefit from the Relaxation Response, everyone can benefit from the Reflection Response. The people in this book who pray and meditate offer some helpful suggestions for others who want to improve their capacity for reflection, whether or not they call it prayer.

Here, then, are some of those suggestions, five habits of highly effective pray-ers. Not everyone in this book uses all of these approaches, and no one should feel any obligation to use all of them. But using some of them can restore a needed perspective to hectic lives:

1. Take a few minutes early in the morning to clear your head, collect your thoughts, and set some goals and priorities for the day. If you exercise regularly, use it as a time to reflect as well.

2. Use cues throughout the day to remind yourself that there is another dimension to life beyond racing from chore to chore, from deadline to deadline, from crisis to crisis. Archbishop Weakland says he prays every time he opens the refrigerator door or a car door. Sometimes it takes just a few seconds to get back our perspective.

3. Take a few seconds to reflect before any confrontation, whether it's an important conversation or dealing with a work problem. Regrouping can help us say the right thing or—what's often more important—avoid saying the wrong thing.

4. Do some reading that helps you think about values, priorities, beliefs, and ways to live better. This may mean the Bible, or spiritual readings, or *The One-Minute Manager*; the important thing is to stimulate reflection.

5. Make notes. Jotting down a note or two can help you retain ideas, insights, and goals that come in a flash during reflection and then easily slip away.

Reflection is a key to well-being. But as with prayer, the real value can be found in behavioral changes. You can pray all day and all night; you can practice the Relaxation Response; you can reflect upon your life. But if you don't become, in Robert Schuller's words, "a really generous and caring person," or if, in Dan Seals's words, you continue to "screw people around," then you haven't prayed at all.

ABOUT THE AUTHOR

JIM CASTELLI, who lives in Northern Virginia, has written about religion for the past twenty-five years. He has written for *Time*, *USA Today*, Gannet News Service, and the *Los Angeles Times* Syndicate.

His books include *The Bishops and the Bomb*, *A Plea for Common Sense: Resolving the Clash Between Religion and Politics*, *The Emerging Parish* (with Joseph Gremillion), and *The American Catholic People* and *The People's Religion* (with George Gallup, Jr.).